Internet Marketing
with WordPress

Use the power of WordPress to target customers,
increase traffic, and build your business

David Mercer

BIRMINGHAM - MUMBAI

Internet Marketing with WordPress

Copyright © 2011 Packt Publishing

First published: November 2011

Production Reference: 1151111

Published by Packt Publishing Ltd.
Livery Place
35 Livery Street
Birmingham B3 2PB, UK.

ISBN 978-1-84951-674-7

www.packtpub.com

Cover Image by Vinayak Chittar (vinayak.chittar@gmail.com)

Credits

Author
David Mercer

Reviewer
Dennis Miller

Acquisition Editor
Robin de Jongh

Technical Editor
Kedar Bhat

Proofreader
Aaron Nash

Indexer
Hemangini Bari

Graphics
Manu Joseph

Production Coordinator
Nilesh Mohite

Cover Work
Nilesh Mohite

About the Author

David Mercer was born in August 1976 in Harare, Zimbabwe. Having always had a strong interest in science, David came into regular contact with computers at university where he graduated "cum laude" with majors in Applied Math and Math.

His technical books are now sold worldwide and have been translated into French, German, Polish, Greek, Spanish, and many more languages. His book on Drupal 6 was reviewed on Slashdot and went on to become a best seller. Mercer's books have also become recommended reading at higher learning institutes such as MIT, and he has a write-up on Wikipedia.

David divides his time between consulting for companies and organizations in a wide variety of industries, helping them to develop and implement cutting edge systems. He also contributes to interesting web-based projects like design-a-webpage (`http://www.design-a-webpage.com`), which allows people to create beautiful, effective landing pages in minutes—absolutely no code or Web experience required.

He also maintains a blog, training, and support site for his readers at `http://www.siteprebuilder.com`. Site prebuilder provides quizzes and exercises that accompany his books, and serves as his primary online presence and contact point.

When he isn't working (which isn't that often), he enjoys playing guitar (generally on stage and unrehearsed) and getting involved in outdoor activities ranging from touch rugby and golf to water skiing and snowboarding.

Acknowledgement

Writing a book consumes much of your focus and time, and without the proper support can become difficult. Fortunately, I enjoy plenty of support in the form of Chris, Bev, and Andrew (my family), my girlfriend Elizabeth, and the people and businesses I work with, who always understand when I have to disappear for days at a time to work on "those books".

It is necessary to also thank my publishers and everyone on the Packt team for providing the resources required to get this book to print.

Finally, I want to thank my readers for allowing me to do something I enjoy. I hope that you will find plenty of value both in the book and in the accompanying exercises.

About the Reviewer

Dennis R. Miller is Director of Marketing and Public Relations at Mansfield University of Pennsylvania. He has more than 35 years, experience in higher education marketing and has spoken widely over the years on marketing and social media. He writes three blogs using WordPress and is the author of the novel "One Woman's Vengeance."

Mansfield University is a small public liberal arts institution in north central Pennsylvania.

Miller is the author of "The Perfect Song" under the pseudonym of "Damon" and most recently, "One Woman's Vengeance" under his own name.

www.PacktPub.com

Support files, eBooks, discount offers, and more

You might want to visit www.PacktPub.com for support files and downloads related to your book.

Did you know that Packt offers eBook versions of every book published, with PDF and ePub files available? You can upgrade to the eBook version at www.PacktPub.com and as a print book customer, you are entitled to a discount on the eBook copy. Get in touch with us at service@packtpub.com for more details.

At www.PacktPub.com, you can also read a collection of free technical articles, sign up for a range of free newsletters and receive exclusive discounts and offers on Packt books and eBooks.

http://PacktLib.PacktPub.com

Do you need instant solutions to your IT questions? PacktLib is Packt's online digital book library. Here, you can access, read and search across Packt's entire library of books.

Why Subscribe?

- Fully searchable across every book published by Packt
- Copy and paste, print, and bookmark content
- On demand and accessible via web browser

Free Access for Packt account holders

If you have an account with Packt at www.PacktPub.com, you can use this to access PacktLib today and view nine entirely free books. Simply use your login credentials for immediate access.

Table of Contents

Preface

It's very difficult to overstate the importance of Internet marketing.

With the advent of powerful and effective tools (like WordPress) that make it easy for anyone in the world to put up a website, it is now more important than ever to carve out a niche for yourself.

The online world requires its own unique set of marketing skills and techniques that, while based loosely on the principles of traditional marketing, require a broader range of knowledge, specialist skills, and plenty of finesse. It's as much art as it is science and is heaps of fun to learn.

Having solid Internet marketing knowledge and skills will enable you to outcompete hundreds of millions of other websites, and potentially enjoy fantastic rewards. This book seeks to give you the real world marketing knowledge and practice that you will need to succeed online.

What this book covers

Chapter 1, Introduction to WordPress Marketing: Get an overview of how traffic moves around the Internet and how to prepare for a new marketing campaign. Learn how Internet marketing is the process of creating content in order to drive targeted traffic to a blog or website and convert it to meet defined business objectives. In addition, if you weren't already familiar with general marketing lingo, you will be.

Chapter 2, Creating Content to Attract the Target Readers: Understand the importance of analyzing your business objectives as well as your target market. Knowing who to write for and how to reach them forms the basis of how to create quality content that can drive traffic, enhance your reputation, and ultimately allow you to meet your business objectives.

Chapter 3, Building Traffic I: Search Engine Optimization: Enjoy a holistic grounding in the fundamentals of SEO. In particular, you should feel that while SEO is an important and integral part of the success of any blog or website, it is not the be all and end all. Adhere to the basic guidelines with the understanding that SEO practices are there because Google and other search engines want to encourage you to create good quality content.

Chapter 4, Building Traffic II: Socializing WordPress: Here you will get a solid grounding in social media. In particular, you will learn how to use each of the major social networks to further your business objectives. Along with providing useful and interesting high quality content, it is also important to contribute to the social networks by getting involved in discussions and debates, following other people, and generally getting your name out there.

Chapter 5, Building Traffic III: Building Relationships: Get a refresher on how to leverage the WordPress community to create relationships and trust that can help to increase your reach and generate traffic. We will also look at how RSS can help to tie people into your site by offering them an easy way to access the main headlines and teasers, how feedburner can be used to monetize and enhance the traffic generated by your feeds, and how to use advertising with caution.

Chapter 6, Converting Traffic: Discover how to leverage your quality content and make it very easy for people so stay within reach of it through RSS, Twitter, Facebook, LinkedIn, and any other appropriate services, and learn how to drastically improve your chances of converting visitors into fans, followers, and customers using powerful landing pages.

Chapter 7, Analyze, Refine, and Repeat: By understanding traffic patterns and using that information to identify weaknesses and strengths in your strategy, you will be able to implement sophisticated and well-tuned marketing campaigns to out-compete your competitors and drive revenue, reach, and success.

Work smart *and* hard, not just hard.

What you need for this book

This book assumes the reader has a basic working knowledge of the WordPress content management system. Coverage is given to both hosted and self-hosted versions of WordPress.

Who this book is for

This book is for anyone who wishes to promote or market their blog, products, or services online through their WordPress blog.

In particular anyone who wishes to learn how to effectively use their blog to market online without requiring a large advertising budget will find plenty of value here.

Conventions

In this book you will find a number of styles of text that distinguish between different kinds of information. Here are some examples of these styles, and an explanation of their meaning.

Code words in text are shown as follows: "Self-hosted WordPress users may want to edit their `robots.txt` file to prevent duplicate content from appearing in Google's index."

Any command-line input or output is written as follows:

```
<ul>
<li style="display:inline;"><a href="path_to_email">
<img src="email_icon_file_url" alt="contact me via email"
  /></a></li>
```

New terms and **important words** are shown in bold. Words that you see on the screen, in menus, or dialog boxes for example, appear in the text like this: "Click on **Connect to Facebook** and then click on **Authorize connection in Facebook** button that appears in the pop up."

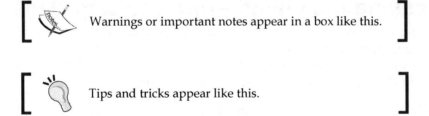

Warnings or important notes appear in a box like this.

Tips and tricks appear like this.

Reader feedback

Feedback from our readers is always welcome. Let us know what you think about this book—what you liked or may have disliked. Reader feedback is important for us to develop titles that you really get the most out of.

To send us general feedback, simply send an e-mail to feedback@packtpub.com, and mention the book title via the subject of your message.

If there is a book that you need and would like to see us publish, please send us a note in the **SUGGEST A TITLE** form on www.packtpub.com or e-mail suggest@packtpub.com.

If there is a topic that you have expertise in and you are interested in either writing or contributing to a book, see our author guide on www.packtpub.com/authors.

Customer support

Now that you are the proud owner of a Packt book, we have a number of things to help you to get the most from your purchase.

Downloading the example code

You can download the example code files for all Packt books you have purchased from your account at http://www.PacktPub.com. If you purchased this book elsewhere, you can visit http://www.PacktPub.com/support and register to have the files e-mailed directly to you.

Accessing the online exercises & quizzes

As with his last book, the author provides an online community focused on improving the skills learned in this book on his website (http://www.siteprebuilder.com). Simply browse to the "Books" section and click on "Interactive Learning" under the appropriate title.

You will be able to consolidate and extend your practical knowledge using the exercises, and test your understanding by taking a series of marked quizzes. In addition, you will enjoy any number of online extras, be able to interact with other readers, and communicate with the author directly.

Errata

Although we have taken every care to ensure the accuracy of our content, mistakes do happen. If you find a mistake in one of our books—maybe a mistake in the text or the code—we would be grateful if you would report this to us. By doing so, you can save other readers from frustration and help us improve subsequent versions of this book. If you find any errata, please report them by visiting http://www.packtpub.com/support, selecting your book, clicking on the **errata submission form** link, and entering the details of your errata. Once your errata are verified, your submission will be accepted and the errata will be uploaded on our website, or added to any list of existing errata, under the Errata section of that title. Any existing errata can be viewed by selecting your title from http://www.packtpub.com/support.

Piracy

Piracy of copyright material on the Internet is an ongoing problem across all media. At Packt, we take the protection of our copyright and licenses very seriously. If you come across any illegal copies of our works, in any form, on the Internet, please provide us with the location address or website name immediately so that we can pursue a remedy.

Please contact us at copyright@packtpub.com with a link to the suspected pirated material.

We appreciate your help in protecting our authors, and our ability to bring you valuable content.

Questions

You can contact us at questions@packtpub.com if you are having a problem with any aspect of the book, and we will do our best to address it.

1
Introduction to WordPress Marketing

A successful WordPress blog or site is one that insinuates itself into the fabric of the Web really well. It contributes to the rich tapestry of interlinked blogs, sites, and social media, and becomes part and parcel of daily life in its particular niche. A good site does not standalone. Instead, it provides a platform for people to find information, become engaged, or be entertained.

Fitting into your niche

Using WordPress gives you a competitive advantage because you can spend more time focusing on creating content and marketing your ideas, products, or services without having to learn how to be a competent programmer.

This is important because there is a complex web of relationships, competition, and creativity that goes into carving out a niche. You will compete directly with some people, collaborate with others, teach still more and, hopefully, learn from others at the same time. In particular, a blog from WordPress.com makes it very easy to engage with your niche because it comes ready-made with virtually everything a modern site needs—including a large and active community of bloggers.

In any given niche, there are already established players, newbies, spammers, bloggers, forums, wannabies, and so on. Much about online success or failure comes down to the *art* of dealing with these different people in a variety of different settings because it is these people who may ultimately recommend or shun you and have a direct bearing on your success or failure.

Internet marketing overview

I don't want to spend too long introducing all the different terms and concepts involved in the field of Internet marketing. I am a firm believer in jumping in and learning to swim—which is why this book is short, sweet, and packed with useful stuff that you can use in the real world.

With that said, it is important that you are at least familiar with the major terms, concepts, and processes I am going to use; and it won't hurt to give you a bird's-eye view of the how, why, what, where, and when of marketing online. You don't need to be a marketing pro to benefit from the straightforward process contained in this book.

The following steps are the overall process we are going to follow:

1. Define business objectives
2. Identify target audience
3. Create content
4. Drive traffic
5. Convert traffic (monetize)
6. Analyze
7. Refine
8. Repeat

This chapter is going to define and explain all the terms used in this list and place them within the context of the Internet and Internet marketing. We will also cover the first two steps here as these are really pre-marketing preparatory steps; in other words, things you need to know before you start marketing at all.

Understanding Internet marketing

The following diagram represents a blog or website within the context of the Internet from a marketing perspective:

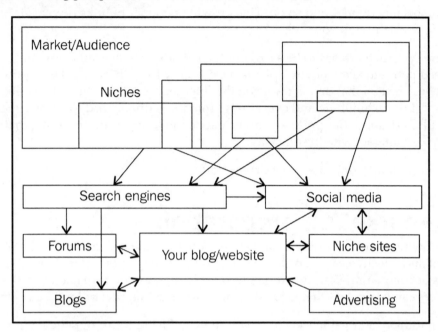

The top layer of this diagram represents the market or audience—all the people out there surfing the web. Note that this mass of people can be broken up into niches, represented by the boxes contained within the overall Market/Audience. A niche can be defined as a specific interest group. For example, some people want to learn about pottery, some enjoy astrophysics.

The diagram has been simplified to show how niche interest groups use search engines and social networks to find the content they are after. Of course, they might well go directly to their favorite forum or niche website without using a search engine, but a large proportion of all traffic goes through search engines and social networks, so this serves as a good model.

Note that different parts of this diagram are related by arrows. In this instance, an arrow represents **traffic**. Traffic is the term used to describe a flow of visitors. Some arrows are one way, indicating that traffic flows from one segment to the other. For example, the arrow between the search engines and your blog is denoted as one way, indicating that traffic comes from the search engines to your site, but not the other way. Two-way arrows mean that traffic, in general, passes either way.

By looking at the web of different arrows, you can see that your site or blog needs to integrate itself into the fabric of the Internet. In order to effectively market a blog, you need to make connections, share content, offer opinions, comment on other people's content, and so on. All of this helps to add links to and from other blogs, forums, social networks, and so on. This growing network of links is what starts traffic flowing through your site.

Like any system, there has to be a driving force that keeps the traffic flowing. Our cars need petrol to keep moving, plants need energy from the sun to keep growing, and so on. The fuel that drives traffic on the Internet is **content**. When I talk about "content", I mean anything and everything from the written word to a YouTube video, PPC ad, audio file, podcast, and just about anything and everything that humans can interact with in someway.

That is important! Content is what drives traffic.

Pre-marketing preparation

The following chapter is going to talk about how to create that content in the most efficient and effective way in order to drive traffic through your blog. However, there is one more important feature of the earlier diagram that we need to talk about before we can begin, and that is identifying your **target market** or **target audience**.

You can think of a target market as one or more defined groups of people who are interested in what you have to say or offer. This is an extremely important concept. While the Internet is a vast place with many millions of people online, inevitably, individuals or small groups of individuals are only interested in certain things at certain times.

Your job as a marketer is to determine which niche interest groups constitute your target market and go after only those people.

 It is a monumental waste of effort marketing to no one in particular.

If you refer back to the earlier diagram, you will note that traffic arrows coming from the market into the search engines and social media sites only came from certain niches and not every niche. This is because I want to make it clear that, depending on the content of your blog or site, only certain niche groups will be interested.

So, before you even begin marketing to anyone, you need to make sure you understand the **value** of what you are offering, and who is likely to want that offering. When I refer to "value", I don't mean, necessarily, in physical dollar and cents terms. You might, for example, offer your opinion on politics or climate change. People may not have to pay to read that opinion, but if they are interested in what you have to say, it holds value for them.

Pre-marketing preparation procedure

The following diagram represents how to prepare for an Internet marketing campaign:

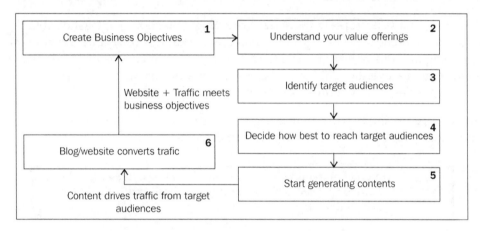

From this diagram, you can see that aside from understanding the value offering (knowing how and why people will derive value from what you offer), it is also important to first create **business objectives** that will ultimately be met by your marketing efforts combined with the blog or site.

In the Internet marketing sense, a business objective is a goal you want your blog to achieve. It could be generating revenue through advertising, it could be getting visitors to sign up to your newsletter, or anything else. When a visitor comes to your website and performs an action that fulfils one or more business objectives, that is called a **conversion**.

A conversion doesn't necessarily have to mean that some form of financial transaction takes place. However, it is important to understand that because marketing is labor intensive, and in some cases financially draining, you should generally frame your efforts within a financial context. That is to say, spend a bit of time working out how best to assign a monetary value to your conversions.

If one of your goals is to sign people up to a newsletter, then you should know how and where you can make money from this newsletter down the line. Perhaps you will market your products or provide links to special offers on your e-commerce site. However, after you monetize that newsletter, you can generally work out how much you expect to earn per sign up. Once the newsletter has been running for some time, you can then make exact calculations based on the number of people signed up and the revenue generated as a result.

For example, if you earn on average $30 in product sales for each new customer, and you gain one new customer for every 100 newsletter signups, then you could work out that $30/100 = 30 cents. This is the value of each newsletter sign up to you. Thinking about those 30 cents helps motivate you to get people signed up.

By ensuring that you properly **monetize** your blog, you should at least be able to pay for the high-end servers required when the marketing efforts pay off and you start getting millions of visitors. The term "monetize" refers to one or more methods used to generate revenue. This could be a result of advertising, affiliate revenue, e-commerce sales, or any number of other things.

Before we discuss the two pre-marketing preparation tasks in a bit more depth, you are now ready for a bird's-eye summary of Internet marketing in its entirety.

 Internet marketing is the process of creating content in order to drive targeted traffic to a blog or website and convert it to meet defined business objectives.

Once our pre-marketing preparation is complete, we are going to dive right in and begin creating content.

Defining business objectives

By clearly defining the expectations for a blog or site, you are in a better position to act coherently towards achieving them, as opposed to writing content in the vague hope people will start reading it and visit regularly.

Business objectives can vary depending on how you intend to convert and monetize traffic. For example, the primary business objective for an e-commerce site is generally to get customers to make a purchase or, more likely, to make repeated purchases. Whereas, the objectives of an affiliate marketer may be to drive targeted, high quality traffic to their affiliate partners.

The abstract case that applies to any blog or site is as follows:

- Attract highly relevant traffic
- Engage that traffic
- Get that traffic to take action *(such as sign-ups, subscriptions, purchases, and so on)*

The last step is one of the most important. For example, you might decide to create a newsletter that keeps readers informed about the latest on-going activities in your particular niche. One of your primary business objectives is, therefore, to get visitors to take action by signing up to the newsletter.

Getting visitors to sign up to a newsletter may require slightly different methods than getting them to donate $100 to a non-profit organization. The point being that effectively planning your objectives can encourage you to precisely analyze visitors' needs and provide focused and relevant content, rather than wasting time on content that doesn't convert.

Finally, an important aspect of any business (whether it is a blog or hardware store) is to become highly regarded and widely known in its niche. Becoming an indispensable part of the fabric of a niche community is immeasurably valuable. As a result, at least one of your business objectives should focus on the blog or site's *standing*. You will learn all about this in *Chapter 4*.

Make sure you visit the exercises for this chapter for a bit of practice with creating business objectives. You can find them in the download pack on www.packtpub.com/support. First click on the selection box as shown in the following screenshot, and select the title of this book:

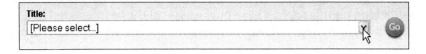

Then enter your e-mail address or log in to your Packt account to download the exercises. Make sure you select the newsletter option to receive news of frequent offers!

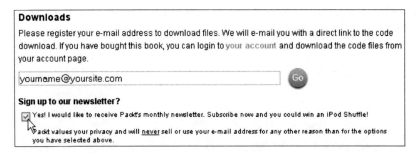

By the way, can you see what the publishers have done here? They are doing what we have been learning in this chapter — getting the reader to take action, monetizing, and engaging with the reader by offering extra content.

Alternatively, you can also go to my site where you have access to marked online quizzes, community involvement, and extras at `www.siteprebuilder.com` and look in the **BOOKS** section.

Identifying the target audience

With a well-defined list of business objectives in hand, you are now ready to work out who you want to reach in order to best meet those goals. In other words, the businesses objectives help determine the target audience.

As it is quite likely that many readers will already have a blog or site up and running at this stage, it is important to state upfront that if, as a result of the research you perform here, you find that your blog or site, in its current form, is not suitable, then it may be necessary to refocus what you have or start a new blog. Don't be afraid to change direction. Rather bite the bullet now than persist with a site that you don't believe will be effective.

Doing a bit of research into who might be interested in your product or service (your target market) can often yield surprising results. For example, you might have a business selling garden furniture with a blog on growing garden plants. The obvious audience for a blog such as this would be home owners as they are most likely to have gardens. What about people who live in apartments?

In all likelihood, gardening services and landscape artists might also be interested in a good quality blog on this topic. These businesses might be interested in a slightly different aspect of gardening, although no doubt there are topics that will appeal to both groups.

Is that all?

What about regional differences? Garden plants in Vermont are not likely to have much appeal to gardeners in New Mexico, unless they are determined to fly in the face of natural selection. Who are you going to cater for?

What about age groups? How many teenagers enjoy gardening work? As unreal as a hardworking teen might sound, I am sure there are one or two lurking around. But do they fit your target market? Probably not, as they are unlikely to own homes and gardens, and therefore won't need garden furniture.

Is income bracket a factor? People who live in apartments may not have the resources or inclination to read up on the fascinating world of garden plants. City dwellers may be very high earners, but still not be interested in gardening. So, urban and sub-urban people may be different in this regard. By considering each and every aspect that goes into making up **ideal visitors**, you can begin to piece together how to present content and information to best meet the stated business objectives.

 Any given audience consists of smaller subgroups. Content should be created to target specific subgroups in order to be as relevant as possible.

In particular, knowing who you are aiming at can help determine the structure of your WordPress blog or site as a whole. Major subgroups of your target market could have content categorized and presented in focused, relevant segments (for example, possibly displayed in the main menu links).

Remember that you can target different market segments organically; focus on one or two major audience subgroups and then branch out once you have additional resources or demand.

Reach the target audience

Knowing who you are catering for is one thing. Knowing how a particular niche industry is already organized is another. It may be that the people you wish to reach tend to use chat groups regularly. Maybe they cluster around one or two large forums, or are widely spread out in smaller communities.

Spend some time learning who the players are. Think about whether they would make a strategic ally or whether they are direct competitors. Find out where the action is. Do people gather at conventions and meet face-to-face, do they hold webinars, or are they disparate and thin on the ground?

Learn what is popular and what isn't. Online communities often have their own flavor or way of doing things. Some, for example, will disallow strong language completely and encourage a tone of respect of moderation. Other communities are barely moderated at all and adopt an "anything goes" attitude.

As your WordPress blog (or the website your blog is integrated with) is going to have to integrate well into the existing networks and communities, it is important to ensure that the content you offer is acceptable within the context of the wider community.

Summary

This introduction has given you an overview of how traffic moves around the Internet, how to define the business objectives that will shape your content, and how to prepare for a new marketing campaign by researching target audiences. In addition, if you weren't familiar with general marketing lingo, you should be now.

The most important thing to take from this chapter is the bird's-eye summary of Internet marketing that was provided in the pre-marketing preparation section. It is worth repeating it here:

 Internet marketing is the process of creating content in order to drive targeted traffic to a blog or website and convert it to meet defined business objectives.

This single sentence encompasses all the major aspects of Internet marketing. While we haven't yet looked at how best to convert traffic, or analyze traffic patterns and refine our marketing, all of these processes will be easy to understand, provided you keep this definition in mind.

As mentioned, the following chapter will discuss how to create great content that will act as the fuel that drives traffic, and ultimately revenue.

2
Creating Content to Attract the Target Readers

The previous chapter made it clear that content is the fuel that drives traffic on the Internet. Traditional businesses that survive without an Internet component might be the only exception to the *content is king* rule. However, if those enterprises actually want to attract business through their website, then even they have to create content; it is not enough to simply have a website and hope it will bring in customers.

Being a WordPress blogger, you are in the wonderful position of having a perfect platform for delivering great content. And, if you know who you are creating content for, what they want, and how to give it to them, then, with perseverance and determination, you will start generating and converting traffic.

The case for content

I know some of you may be feeling a bit frustrated with the suggestion that creating heaps of content is the way to generate business and revenue from your site. It may not be immediately obvious why it is so important to spend time away from traditional marketing, advertising, and other business activities. Would it not be better to spend more time actually trying to generate sales, sell advertising, or marketing products?

The fact is — **Creating content is marketing!**

Putting in the hours to create content is much easier when you adopt the attitude that content is marketing. Every time you sit down to write something, you are doing so with the express intent to generate revenue.

As you will see from the rest of this chapter, we are not simply creating content because it is nice to have a full blog. Every single word you write will be tailored precisely to further the business objectives defined in *Chapter 1*. Every hour you put into making focused, relevant, and engaging content will provide a greater **Return On Investment** (**ROI**) than most other online activities.

The best thing about it is that content is the gift that keeps on giving. Once it is up on your blog or site, it will keep generating traffic through organic searches, keep being referenced by other people, and keep contributing to your SEO and PageRank for a really long time to come.

The most important skill you can take away from this chapter is the ability to create high quality, relevant, and targeted content. Let us look at how to make that content useful, engaging, and conversation worthy and what its benefits are.

Understanding content

Armed with the knowledge (from *Chapter 1*) of who we are writing content for and why, it is now time to begin creating content that will serve as the basis for everything else that is to come.

Content is the glue that binds your site to the rest of the Internet, and binds visitors to your WordPress blog. It is the basis upon which everything you want to achieve rests. By producing good content that is of value to the target market, you are creating the opportunity to build a community of people who serve not only as potential customers but also as an army of marketers.

 Lots of great quality content turns your site into a traffic magnet!

Content works by:

- Providing the search engines with something to index and display in results
- Stimulating and encouraging debate
- Establishing your reputation as a leader
- Building trust with potential customers
- Helping to integrate the blog or site into the fabric of its particular niche
- Providing reference material for other content (for example, other bloggers will quote your work if they feel it is of value to their readers)

In all these cases, the value you derive from the content itself is both long term and cumulative. The more content you have, the more:

- Readers you get
- Back links you get
- You are talked about
- Your reputation is enhanced
- Your popularity increases
- Trust you build
- Revenue you generate

Without content, a blog or site is nothing more than an online business card—and it will never be anything more than that.

Creating content

The following chapter is devoted solely to **Search Engine Optimization (SEO)**, which has a lot to do with the content you create. Accordingly, this section will talk more about how to deliver content for human eyeballs—as opposed to the more technical aspects of creating SEO enhanced content.

Content, in this context, doesn't necessarily mean the written word. It can be any type of media. Anything that goes on your website for people to watch, read, or hear is content. In fact, images and video are steadily becoming the most popular way of presenting information—mainly because visual content is often quicker and easier to digest than the written word.

That is not to say we should spend all our time making videos. What it means is that whenever it adds value to present something graphically, do so. For example, industrial experts often create short video clips highlighting the major points of a thesis or presentation.

In whatever format you choose to present content, there are a few things to keep in mind.

Quality content

When I use the term "quality", I am not referring to the academic merits of the writing. Instead I am specifically talking about content that gives the reader something of value. It could be a laugh; it could be information that they need; it could be a new idea. Whatever it is, good quality content gives the reader the sense that they have gotten something out of the deal—as opposed to wasting their time.

Creating quality content is of paramount importance when it comes to building a good reputation. People will come to trust your content. This trust is manifested in back links, blog postings, references, and all sorts of other goodies. A blog or site that only has great quality content, albeit a small amount, is far more likely to attract repeat visits than one that doesn't provide any real value—even though it may have lots of content.

As corroboration, there are a lot of webmasters that find original content from other sites and use computer algorithms to paraphrase it. This "new" content is then posted to their own blog or site. The idea is that the paraphrased content is perceived as original by Google, and so their blog or site's PageRank is given a boost because they regularly post "original" content.

None of these sites could ever be described as popular in any meaningful sense of the word. The problem is that computer driven paraphrasing often leads to confusing or obfuscated content. Human readers can spot this junk immediately and simply ignore the site, even if Google can't. The site never builds any standing where it counts most—the online community.

Engaging content

Content that is of high quality is not necessarily engaging. A well constructed and accurate thesis may be extremely well written and researched, but dry and bland— even for other academics. However, with a bit of effort and imagination, the very same thesis could be converted into an exciting treatise on the subject in question.

There are ways of presenting content so that it is fun, quick, and easy to read.

Writing engaging content is as much art as science but there are a couple of important ground rules for online content. Always be:

- **Simple**—if something confuses readers they will leave, and you will lose potential income.
- **Clear**—know what you want to write about before you start. Get your point across without obfuscating the issue.

- **Concise** – get straight down to business without adding anything unnecessary.
- **Imaginative** – be fun, quirky, unusual, brilliant… something, anything; but **not** bland and boring.

A good way to help develop your own style is to look at what other people have done and take inspiration from them, learning from their style, not copying it. For example, it is popular practice to create top ten lists of content. Lists are something that everyone is familiar with. People know what to expect when they click on a link saying "Top ten highest grossing movies of all time".

An article covering exactly the same information, but entitled "Statistically significant revenue generators in the film industry" is less likely to attract the same amount of attention, even though they talk about the same thing, more or less. It is just not that engaging.

Lists in themselves are a style of writing that can exhibit all the previously mentioned ground rules for creating engaging content. There is a lot to be said for creating easily digestible information in a format people recognize. This doesn't necessarily mean you should go away and create multitudes of top-ten lists, but you can let this influence your writing style.

In other words, you don't have to turn your content into a load of gimmicky headlines, but get into the habit of presenting content with a unique voice that adheres to these guidelines.

Creating a stir with link bait

As you will see in the coming chapters, good content that is conversation worthy or newsworthy can help to drive traffic to a site or blog. Many successful marketers mix up their normal content with link bait. **Link bait** is any content that is specifically created to cause a stir. It can be something that is incredibly funny, unreal, insensitive, inflammatory, or anything else that will get people talking and referencing it.

The term "link bait" has garnered a bit of negative press because, like almost every aspect of online marketing, some people have implemented it unethically. There is nothing wrong with writing an article specifically to grab people's attention – that's the nature of marketing itself; however, it is important you do so responsibly.

 Link bait content should adhere to the same standards of quality as all other content on your blog.

If the purpose of your blog is to be a respected resource on political debate, then it is probably not a good idea to use insensitive, racist, sexist, or otherwise inflammatory link bait. In this instance, what you gain in bad press you lose in bad press. If the purpose of your blog is to challenge people's beliefs about something, then by all means go with an inflammatory statement because it won't harm your reputation.

The safest option is to use your imagination to come up with new and cool things. Take a look at the following article about how a logo design company gained thousands of visitors (and many incoming links) by asking people to redesign BP's logo after the deepwater horizon oil spill:

```
http://www.searchengineoptimisation.org/bp-oil-disaster-excellent-
link-bait-example/
```

If your link bait is based on something topical, you can really garner people's interest. They might well share it with a few friends because it is worth a chuckle and relevant to them.

 Every time someone shares a post with their friends, or references it from their own blog, the posting (and by extension the site) attracts more links back to it.

Turning every post into link bait runs the risk of making your blog or site seem gimmicky. While link bait is a great way to generate good traffic and links, it should be used as a tool to complement your mainstream content. For example, if you are positioned as a financial industry expert, then most of your content will be about cutting-edge news and information, not about how to sabotage your colleague's stock monitor.

Reach bait

If you haven't heard of reach bait before, then it is because I have only recently coined the term. **Reach bait** is the same as link bait in many respects but differs greatly in how it is applied. Whereas link bait is created with the intention of generating buzz and hype, reach bait is designed to be attractive to individuals or small groups of bloggers or industry experts.

"Reach" is the term used to describe the number of people you can expose to your content. It is extremely important to build reach. The greater your reach, the more the Internet works for you as more people see what you have done and can act on it. No matter who you are, you should always be looking to expand your reach.

Naturally, content is a great way to build reach with time. But, it can be frustrating to write a great blog or post and only have a few people read it because you don't have a huge following on Twitter or LinkedIn. Content does build reach, but it can be a slow and painstaking job. This is where the concept of reach bait can help.

By writing content that is in some way very attractive to other people with greater reach, it is possible to convince them to post your content on their sites, tweet about it, or discuss it in some way. The idea being that you can leverage the reach of other, bigger players to expose your content to a much larger audience.

Every bit of successful reach bait you create adds the reach of whoever posts the content to that of your own. It is a great way to leapfrog the traditional gradual increase in reach. In addition, followers of other bloggers who are exposed to your reach bait are also more likely to start following you as, by default, your content came to them through someone they already trust.

Summary

In this chapter, we saw how content is absolutely crucial in providing a platform from which a blog or site can integrate into the community and build trust, reputation, and high quality traffic.

The most important point to take away, and one that bears repeating here, is that:

 Creating content is marketing!

By ensuring that you look at the task of creating content as integral to the online marketing process, you will be self-motivated to consistently and persistently create content because it is vital for your online success.

With the more human aspects of content creation behind us, we can now focus on the more technical aspects of delivering and disseminating content using a variety of different techniques and mediums.

As with the previous chapter, remember to ensure that you complete any exercises and quizzes available.

3
Building Traffic I: Search Engine Optimization

I am probably going to cause no small amount of wailing and gnashing of teeth by adopting a slightly unconventional approach to the topic of **Search Engine Optimization (SEO)** by saying that it is really not something you should lose any sleep over. SEO is not hard. It doesn't require you to spend vast sums of money on specialist services who promise to get your blog to the top of search engine results.

In fact, as we will see in the coming chapters, WordPress comes with many SEO features built into the design. This allows you to focus more on the content-related SEO features as opposed to more technical, software, and design-related aspects, such as page aliasing. Before I get ahead of myself, let us take a quick look at the definition of SEO.

 SEO is the process of enhancing a site or blog's perceived importance in search engines so that it appears higher up in **SERPs (Search Engine Results Pages)**.

The benefit of appearing at the top of a search is that statistically you are more likely to get traffic. If you have ever done a search on Google or any of the other major search engines, you will know that more often than not what you need is on the first page. By applying SEO techniques, it is possible to improve (not guarantee) the chances of a website appearing near the top of searches relating to the content you create.

Search engines index content. That content is then available for display in their search results. Search engines try to provide highly relevant results to their users, and so the subject of your content plays an important role in where, when, and to whom it is shown.

Relevant content is so important to search engines that it is fair to say—SEO is an implicit result of creating high quality content.

In other words, by creating high quality, relevant, focused, and engaging content, as outlined in the previous chapter, your site will automatically enjoy many SEO benefits. However, good content is not everything. We will also take a look at other techniques and WordPress features you can use to enhance your blog's SEO throughout this chapter.

Understanding Internet search

The Internet would not be the force it is at present without powerful search engines such as Google. Incidentally, as Google is by some margin the most popular search engine, and therefore the most important, we will use it for our discussion throughout the rest of the book.

It is critically important for search engines to provide relevant results; otherwise, people will use another service. A search engine's survival, therefore, comes down to how efficiently they can provide results that best meet a user's requirement. In order to survive, a search engine needs to do the following two things very well:

- Index as much content as possible
- Return highly relevant results

By indexing as much online content as possible and making it available to everyone, Google allows people to find what they are after. But there's a catch. As there is so much content online, Google needs a way to decide which content is the *best* and most likely to give people what they want.

These dual pressures on the search engines are transmitted to bloggers and webmasters in the form of the **PageRank** algorithm. PageRank, specifically a Google term, is used by all search engines (in one form or another) and is a measure of the importance of a given web page. The higher the PageRank, the greater the perceived importance, and the nearer to the top of the search results a page appears.

As Google wants to return the best possible results, it ranks all the pages in its index and uses PageRank as an important component in this calculation. But, it is also in the search engines' interest to help people create high-quality content as this also helps to return better results.

Google clearly outlines and explains much of what you
need to know about SEO in their Webmaster guidelines at
`http://googlewebmastercentral.blogspot.`
`com/2008/11/googles-seo-starter-guide.html`.

Google wants you to create high quality, relevant content and it tells you how to do
it. Adhering to these guidelines, and using a couple of additional neat tricks, will
provide everything you need to ensure you are squeezing every last drop of SEO
goodness from your site.

It is a beautiful, interlocking system of mutual advantage based on one thing—high
quality, relevant content. Do it right and everyone benefits. The user finds what
they are after on your site, and is ultimately satisfied with the search engine that
sent them to you; the search engine is happy with you for helping them to provide a
quality result; you are happy that the search engine sent the user to you, and allowed
you to generate some revenue from that traffic.

SEO for WordPress sites

Recall from *Chapter 2* that content should be *relevant, simple, clear,* and *concise.* I am
going to also add "fresh" to this list. It is not sufficient to write one article and hope
that Google will place your blog at the top of the SERPs. Content must be fresh. In
other words, it has to be added and updated regularly. If it is, Google recognizes
your blog as a dynamic and active source of content, and will continually update its
index with material from your blog. If not, your blog will slide into obscurity.

These five attributes are ones that search engines want to encourage, as content
having these attributes is ultimately the easiest for users to understand and derive
value from. The guidelines that are supplied by Google are ultimately informed by
these principles and designed to encourage (if not enforce) their application.

I recommend, in addition to the guidelines mentioned earlier, you also browse the
Google Webmaster guidelines page found at `https://www.google.com/support/`
`webmasters/bin/answer.py?answer=35769`.

Site structure

The structure of your site or blog is important. It should be clear and easy to
navigate. This means there should be no **orphaned** pages. In other words, every page
should be linked (reachable) from another part of the site, otherwise Google may not
find it and index it and no **SEO value** can come from it.

However, orphaned pages do have some uses. We will see more about how multiple landing pages, which are temporary and often orphaned, can be used to maximize conversions in *Chapter 7*.

The following are some guidelines that will help you to maintain an easy-to-understand site structure:

- Create meaningful and descriptive categories and tags
- Use pages, not posts, for important information about your site, such as "about us" pages
- Ensure that important pages are easy to find (in menus, links, widgets, and so on)
- Ensure that your menu(s) are logical and easy to understand
- Ensure that you use internal links to cross-reference important pages

Effectively, your site should be structured in such a way that visitors are funneled towards conversions. This means that your site must be intuitive to use so that people don't get confused by following menu links that say one thing but deliver another, for example.

So important is site structure that WordPress.com comes with built-in XML sitemap features. Simply go to `http://www.your-domain.com/sitemap.xml` to view your blog's sitemap. WordPress.org users can simply download a sitemap plugin such as Google XML sitemaps at `http://wordpress.org/extend/plugins/google-sitemap-generator`.

Sitemaps are XML documents that help search engines understand the structure of your blog and index it accordingly. A good sitemap will help Google to find posts and pages more easily and get them into its index—obviously, something that is critical for SEO. With a sitemap in hand, your next step is to give it to Google (and any other search engines you think are important) through its Webmaster tools service.

Google Webmaster tools (`https://www.google.com/webmasters`) are one of the best ways to keep in touch with how the search engines are treating your site or blog. This service provides a lot of helpful information on whether or not Google is indexing the site properly, search performance, keywords and phrases, malware, crawl errors, and so on. Complete coverage of Google Webmaster tools as well as information about adding XML sitemaps is given in *Chapter 7*.

Page structure

As important as the overall structure of your blog or site is, the structure of each page also plays a crucial role in SEO. Right from the domain name of the site down to the wording of each link make a concerted effort to ensure that everything is accurate and relevant to the content itself.

Fortunately, WordPress does a great job of ensuring that much of the structural SEO requirements of a site are automatically built in. For example, the title of a post, which you as the author of the content should ensure clearly describes the content itself, is added to the page title and the URL (as you can see from the blog post entitled **Cisco To Buy Comptel's Axioss Software Assets For $31 Million In Cash** at `http://techcrunch.com/2011/08/22/cisco-to-buy-comptels-axioss-software-assets-for-31-million-in-cash/`):

A search on Google for the phrase **Cisco To Buy Comptel's Axioss** returns this blog post as the number one result, as shown in the following screenshot:

The important thing to note here is how the structure of the page has affected the results. The search phrase is highlighted by Google wherever it appears in the results page. We can see that this has occurred once in the title of the page, once in the content summary, and once in the URL—giving this phrase a total of three occurrences out of four lines of search result space.

You can understand why Google and other search engines are almost compelled to put a page like this near the top of the results for that particular search—the search query appears everywhere in the result. OK, so techcrunch.com is a huge site already with plenty of authority, but that just goes to show what you can achieve by using WordPress's ready-made SEO-friendly features within your blog's page structure correctly.

Keywords and phrases

It is important to use the words and phrases you think people might use when searching for your content. My blog would probably not rank too highly under "IT services for bloggers and webmasters" (for which it appears first on Google), if I had given it a tagline such as "Using IT to help people do what they want with their blogs".

As potential clients and readers are precisely the type of people who are searching for things like "IT services for bloggers" or "IT services for webmasters", it makes sense to embed these phrases into the content so that Google understands exactly what the subject of the content is all about.

Apart from the domain, title, and URL of a web page, it is also important to use keyword and phrases within:

- Headings (H1, H2, H3, H4, and H5 in descending order of importance)
- Tags

- Categories
- Link text
- Alternate text or Alt attribute, as well as the Title attribute of images

While these particular aspects of your content hold more sway in terms of making certain keywords and phrases more SEO visible to the search engines, it is also important to simply use your keywords and phrases in a natural way within plain content. Don't stuff your content with keywords at the expense of readability. It is more important that humans can read your content than the search engines.

Please ensure you complete the exercises provided in the download pack for important, additional practice on how to research and use the most effective SEO keywords and key phrases using the Google keywords tool.

Tags and categories

The following screenshot shows the **Edit Post** page for a bit of content about using the topulo.us prediction platform (http://www.topulo.us) as a means of driving traffic and affiliate income through interesting and insightful predictions:

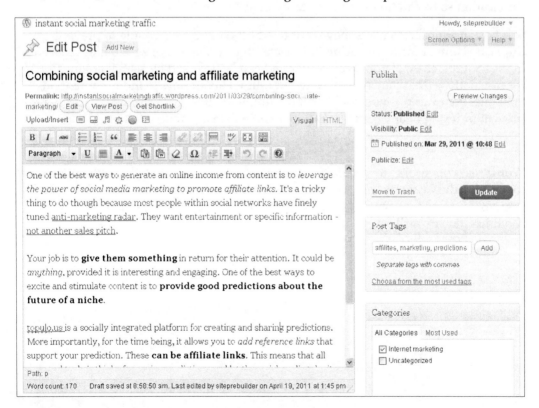

Note in particular that there is a widget (on the right-hand side of the page) that allows for Post Tags. Tags are any words or phrases that best describe the content. They are a really useful way of providing navigation for users by topic or interest. If I go to a blog and read a great article on SEO, the chances are I will click on the SEO tag for that post to see what else has been written on the subject.

Categories on the other hand should be quite familiar to you already, and can be used to separate content into logical groupings. It is easy to create a few categories and add each post to the appropriate ones. For example, the earlier screenshot shows that the topulo.us post is assigned to the **Internet marketing** category (bottom right widget).

Be aware that creating multiple categories and classifying the same content multiple times can lead to Google thinking that there is a lot of duplicate content on your site. This is because, say, your post will appear on the front page and additionally in each category page it is present in. Over categorizing content also makes it harder for users to understand the structure of your site.

Google does allow for a certain amount of duplication because it understands that not all duplication is malicious. However, it may penalize your site for excessive duplication so be careful not to over categorize content.

Self-hosted WordPress users may want to edit their `robots.txt` file to prevent duplicate content from appearing in Google's index. The `robots.txt` file is placed in the root directory of your web server and can be accessed by search engines for instructions (that they may or may not follow) about how to index content on your site. For example, you could add the following line to your `robots.txt` file to prevent indexing of any content that appears in the `tag` archive folder:

```
Disallow: /tag/
```

WordPress.com users are unable to edit the `robots.txt` file to tell search engines not to re-index duplicate content. However, as mentioned, Google and the other search engines do allow for some duplicate content without imposing penalties, so you should be fine regardless.

Document structure

When planning to write a blog post or article, make sure the content is logically structured and broken up into organized, intuitive sections. It is also an accepted practice to add a visual aspect to written content to help give a quick, easy to understand indication of what the content is about. Most often, visual clues are supplied by an image, but video is also useful.

Naturally, being a web document, we also want to make sure that we make intelligent use of links to help funnel traffic to where we need it to go. Links are hugely important, regardless of whether they are internal links (linking one page on your site to another), or external links (linking a page on your site to or from another site).

Let us take a look at the three most important aspects of a web document's structure, namely headings, images, and links.

Headings

Don't be afraid to use headings regularly. Each blog post can have multiple headings provided they contribute to the clarity and structure of the document itself.

Take a look at the following example article on marketing explained with reference to cows—`http://www.siteprebuilder.com/content/online-marketing-explained-reference-cows`. Note how each marketing term is presented in a heading; this tells Google that this is an important part of the document. Google is then more likely to rank this page highly on these terms.

Images

As Google can't actually interpret and understand images, it needs a bit of guidance from you. After all, you are the one adding an image to your content, so you are in the best position to describe it. Image title and Alternate text can be added to any image during upload, or edited any time after. For example, the following screenshot shows the WordPress image edit form:

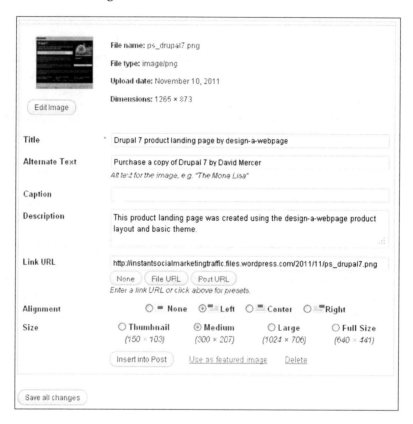

The **Title** gives the image a descriptive name and the **Alternate Text** is displayed in the browser in the event the image itself is unavailable (some browsers display it as a tooltip). Google uses the title and alternative text information to understand what the image is about and this can help the image to appear in a number of different search results.

Every single image you add to a site should be properly described using key words and phrases for SEO enhancement.

Links

Links should always, as a rule, use descriptive text that describes the target content or page. The following screenshot shows the **Add New Link** dialog:

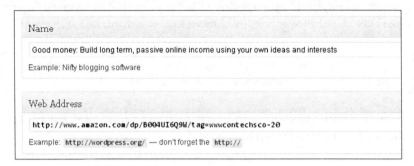

The new link then appears on the site as shown in the following screenshot:

This not only makes it abundantly clear to the reader what to expect by clicking on the link, but it also gives Google a heads-up on what to expect from the link itself. Google can then use this text to rank the target page for the keywords in the link itself. In other words, the good money course landing page on Siteprebuilder.com is credited with keywords such as "Good money" and "online income".

Never create links that read "**Click here**" as this doesn't mean anything to Google, and may also be confusing to humans. In addition, Google recommends that you don't turn entire paragraphs into links—keep link text short and meaningful.

Also, if you do end up swapping links with friends and colleagues, make sure that you vary the content of the link text. Handing out a thousand links that are all exactly the same makes Google suspicious of dubious linking practices and you may be penalized.

Dos and don'ts

People often stray from the bounds of common sense in order to gain a competitive advantage in the world of SEO. I think it is important to caution against getting too caught up in advanced, highly competitive SEO practices. The over-riding point you need to remember is as follows (I know I have said it before, but it is important):

 The most powerful SEO practice is to produce high-quality, relevant content consistently and persistently!

With that said, there are some dos and don'ts that you can use to ensure that you aren't needlessly losing SEO benefits.

Do

- Choose a relevant domain name
- Create relevant page and post titles
- Use SEO keywords and phrases in link text
- Create interesting content that is highly relevant to your niche
- Use Alt and Title attributes for images
- Use keywords naturally and where appropriate
- Encourage people to link to your site or blog
- Encourage people to quote your content with attribution
- Comment on other blogs and websites (preferably using a signature with a link back to your own site or blog)
- Encourage people to comment on your posts

Don't

- Create duplicate content
- Copy or scrape other people's content
- Link to too many external sites on every page
- Stuff your content with keywords
- Write content for search engines — only write for humans
- Disguise links
- Create pages with little or no content
- Use images, flash, video without creating some text
- Post media (video, audio, presentation, and so on) without making every effort to describe it sensibly

Remember, that one of the factors that Google takes into account when assigning a PageRank for your site is longevity. Newer sites aren't automatically assigned super-high PageRanks. In fact, sites that have been around for a long time are more likely to be high quality, so they are the ones that get a PageRank boost. Recently, however, Google has downgraded the importance of this particular metric, though it is still a factor.

Incidentally, there are online services that allow you to check your Google PageRank. Just do a Google search for "Online pagerank" and pick any of the sites that show up, or alternatively install the Google toolbar which includes a Pagerank checker.

Finally, it is worth re-iterating the following:

> If you are working on a blog or site that is a true reflection of your interests and passions, then you will have the stick-to-it-ness to contribute to it consistently over a long period of time.

Eventually you will build up an enviable body of super-high quality and SEO enhanced content that will work for you day and night, even when you are lying on a beach sipping Pina Coladas.

Summary

This chapter provided a holistic grounding in the fundamentals of SEO. In particular, you should feel that while SEO is an important and integral part of the success of any blog or website, it is not the be all and end all. Adhere to the basic guidelines with the understanding that SEO practices are there because Google and other search engines want to encourage you to create good quality content.

After gaining an understanding of how Internet search works and why the search engines take certain factors into account when deciding how to rank pages, we saw that by following a few simple steps it is possible to maximize the chances of appearing high up in SERPs.

Finally, a comprehensive list of SEO dos and don'ts provided an easy-to-understand set of guidelines that will ensure you don't lose out on any SEO goodness unnecessarily.

4
Building Traffic II: Socializing WordPress

If you were under the impression that having great content was sufficient to build a successful site, think again. There are no two ways about it. Either be social, or prepare for disappointment. It is absolutely imperative to get people to link to your content, comment on your blog, connect with you, tweet about you, follow you, discuss things you say, talk about your site, and anything else you can think of—you won't find a single popular blog that does not implement several different social features.

Social media and social networks are so important and so prevalent they have led some experts to call the Internet the Social Web. Operating a website without social engagement is like a shop set up in the remote wilderness where no one can find it. In other words, it makes it really hard for word to spread.

Incidentally, the definition of **social media** is:

"Content designed to be disseminated through social interaction, created using highly accessible and scalable publishing techniques".

Talking of which, despite all the advantages and incredible potential of the Internet, the best form of marketing is still word of mouth. Word of mouth no longer applies in the literal sense, but if people see a tweet from a friend, or a post on Facebook, then they are far more likely to click through to that page than if they see the exact same thing shown by someone they don't know.

 Social media is the online equivalent of word of mouth!

However, there is a downside to all of this. As there is so much social content flying around all the time, the attention an individual will pay to each social message is less than he/she would pay to an actual verbal word-of-mouth recommendation. This makes it even more important to target only the groups that will be interested in your blog. In other words the target audience you defined in *Chapter 1*. If you don't you may find yourself spending hours online for no particular benefit.

By ensuring that your content is socially integrated, you give it the best chance of being picked up not by tens or hundreds, or even thousands of people, but millions, and sometimes tens of millions — depending on the market size of your niche. Creating a bit of media that goes viral and is seen by millions of people can completely change the face of your enterprise in the space of a day or two.

Exciting, isn't it?

Understanding social networks

The chances are you already use one or more social networks such as Facebook, Google+, or LinkedIn. If you have used more than one, you are probably aware that there are distinct differences between them. Each of the large, successful networks has filled its own niche, making it distinct from all the others.

Each network, in turn, caters for people operating in different areas of their lives, that is, business, hobbies, friends, dating, and so on. These differences in how the various networks are used and by whom, create lots of choices when it comes to finding and targeting markets for your content (media).

It is worth noting that for all social networks — connecting with people who have little in common with what you do and are trying to achieve will dilute the effectiveness of your content, and waste your valuable time.

Before we go ahead and start exploring how to share content on these networks, there are a few important things to remember. Make sure to keep these in the back of your mind at all times:

- Networks consist of real, individual humans; they are not an amorphous mass of faceless traffic
- Each network is sub-divided into smaller interest groups
- People on different social networks are there for specific reasons
- Each network has its own way of doing things — a kind of community flavour

The point of this list is to highlight the fact that while you still follow precisely the same procedure for creating content and still have to identify target markets and create content designed specifically to attract and convert those people, you now have to take into account the **social context**.

Writing content aimed at a LinkedIn group can probably have a strong business bias, as that is what LinkedIn is all about. However, you might have to tweak the content based on which particular group you are targeting. For example, writing an article on pancake mix and sharing it with the hypothetical 'Association of Bakers' would focus more on the technical aspects of creating the mix, whereas writing the same article for the League of Discerning Gourmands would focus more on the qualities and taste of the mix.

Different aspects of a single subject, therefore, interest different social groups, requiring the same fundamental topic (pancake mix, in this case) to take into account social context. Getting the exact same message across on Facebook would no doubt require a complete rewrite in order to make it palatable to groups or individuals hanging out there.

While we are on the subject of different networks, let us take a look at the main ones. Remember that there are plenty of other networks that may be very suited to your particular niche.

Facebook

Facebook is the largest social network on the planet, with more than half a billion users spread across the globe. It represents a wide range of marketing opportunities above and beyond your own personal network of friends.

However, I think it is important to note that there is so much to do on Facebook that you will have to think carefully about where best to expend effort. It is quite possible to spend all day, every day, building up a following on Facebook to the exclusion of your own site or blog.

My advice is to adopt the attitude that Facebook is an important component of your WordPress blog or site marketing. In other words, you will need to set aside time on a regular basis to keep your Facebook presence fresh and interesting, but not as much time as you spend creating content and marketing your primary WordPress site.

You should consider the following list of things while working on Facebook. Remember, it is important not to expect too much, too soon from Facebook. Treat your marketing initiative as an incremental process. The benefits will accrue with time as you build more trust and followers. Refer to the exercises for this chapter in the download pack or on Site prebuilder in order to manually work through each option:

- Create a fan page for your blog, site, or business
- Join relevant niche interest groups
- Create regular events
- Create relationships by contributing to other fan pages

Once you have a presence on Facebook in the form of a fan page or group, the aim is to get as many people as possible (preferably those who form a part of your target market) to like and share that presence. The more people like what you offer the greater your Facebook reach becomes. This is particularly useful because it is very easy to engage people on the Facebook platform.

Automatic Facebook access to WordPress

WordPress has facilities to update your personal profile with headlines from your blog.

Remember that this may not be appropriate if your blog specifically focuses on business matters as your friends may not appreciate having to read about your work.

The following section deals with the WordPress Publicize plugin that ships with hosted sites by default. People using self-hosted WordPress sites will either have to wait for the Publicize plugin to be made available to them or consider using alternative plugins such as SharePress (http://wordpress.org/extend/share/pubins/sharepress).

WordPress asks for a number of access permissions, including access to your basic information (which is generally not a problem), permission to post to your wall, and access to your data anytime. If you are not comfortable with handing out these permissions to WordPress, then skip this section.

Assuming you do want to share posts on your Facebook account, go to **Sharing** under **Settings** in the WordPress dashboard.

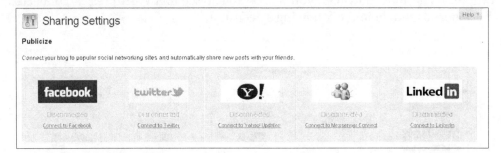

Click on **Connect to Facebook** and then click on **Authorize connection in Facebook** button that appears in the pop up. This will take you through to the Facebook authorization page as shown in the following screenshot:

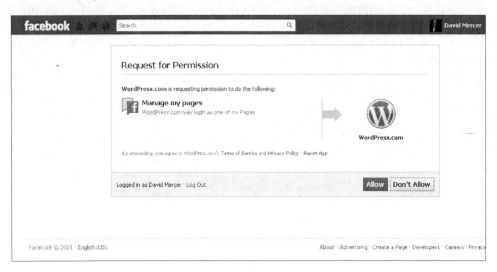

Click on **Allow** to accept this request and any other permission requests that follow. Once you have finished, you will be redirected back to the **Sharing** page on WordPress. This time, however, you will be able to see that WordPress is connected to Facebook, as shown in the following screenshot:

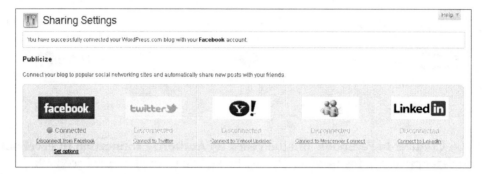

With this connection in place, any new post from your blog goes straight to your Facebook home page and is visible to anyone who has access to your Facebook profile. You will notice too that there is a new **Publicize** option on the WordPress **Add New Post** page:

As soon as the post is published to WordPress, it is simultaneously published to your Facebook account where it can be liked and commented on:

Note that the custom message that I typed into the **Publicize** form shows up as the text posted to Facebook. This gives you a bit more control over how you present your content (as opposed to always having to use the title of the post, which may not be exactly what you want). Most importantly, there is a link back to your blog in the form of the **Read original post** at the bottom right. This is a great traffic generator if you can get enough people interested.

LinkedIn

LinkedIn recently crossed the 100 million user mark and is still growing. Unlike Facebook, LinkedIn focuses specifically on social interaction for business purposes. It is a great place to put up your CV, go job hunting, connect with current and past colleagues, and find and interact with specific types of business people.

Like other social networks, people you are connected to can view the stream of content you create on their LinkedIn home page. The temptation is, therefore, to increase your reach by connecting with as many people as possible. In the case of LinkedIn, it is far better to:

- Fill out your profile completely
- Connect with people you already know (past and current workmates, classmates, and so on)
- Join relevant industry groups
- Connect only to unknown people if they have a clear alignment of interests or are potentially useful from a strategic point of view

In particular, joining relevant industry groups (some of which measure in the hundreds of thousands of members) gives you the opportunity to engage in debate and start your own discussions. You will find that most groups have a number of rules and regulations in place that govern the type of content that is acceptable there. In general, self-promotion is strictly frowned upon, so take a few moments to read up on each group's particular set of rules before you start contributing.

Twitter

Promoting your own blog or website content can be handled directly by WordPress using the same procedure for Twitter as we used for Facebook. Twitter is a micro-blogging service that allows people to share short messages of up to 140 characters at a time. It has become popular because it is one of the quickest and best ways to share snippets of information with a wide audience. By posting regularly to Twitter and following other relevant people, it is possible to gain a large following and really improve your reach.

Unlike other networks, however, Twitter can be used more freely and broadly. No one is going to mind if you post a tweet about your latest product—as they would if you did the same thing on LinkedIn. That is not to say you have carte blanche to self-promote like crazy. No one is going to be interested enough to follow you unless you provide great and interesting content.

 Without followers, you have no reach; and without reach, Twitter is essentially useless from a marketing point of view.

When it comes to using Twitter effectively, there are a number of points to keep in mind:

- Provide fresh, interesting, and relevant content
- Tweet about interesting things (even if they aren't specifically about you)
- Share useful links
- Follow other people
- Comment on other people's tweets
- Tweet about future events or upcoming deals, sales, or specials
- Promote your own blog or website content by sharing your post headlines through your Twitter account

Point five—Comment on other people's tweets—is really important. You will find that a lot of people are pumping out a lot of tweets. There is so much information whizzing around that you will never be able to read everything coming from the people you are following. But, taking the time to comment on as many posts, by as many different people as possible, will make you stand out and this will encourage more people to follow you.

The final point—*Promote your own blog or website content*—can be handled directly by WordPress using the same procedure for Twitter as we used for Facebook a bit earlier in this chapter.

Integrate your blog with Twitter

If you haven't already, go ahead and **Connect** your WordPress blog with Twitter using the Publicize plugin (WordPress.org users will have to make use of an alternative Twitter plugin such as Simple Twitter Connect at `http://wordpress.org/extend/pugins/simple-twitter-connect` or simply use the twitter share button to manually tweet new posts). With that in place, new blog posts will automatically be made available in Twitter, and it is then up to you to set aside a bit of time every day to grow your network by making additional tweets, commenting on other people's tweets, and following other people.

> **Twitter hash tags**
>
> Be sure to check out the exercises for this chapter in the download pack or on Site prebuilder to learn about hash tags that can help leverage the power of tweets to find a larger audience.

Digg & Reddit

Digg (`http://www.digg.com`) and Reddit (`http://www.reddit.com`) are social news networks. Anyone can post links to either of these services and if they are interesting, then it may go viral and drive huge traffic volumes to your blog. There is a catch, however. Both Digg and Reddit community members are often anti-marketing. If they feel that you have sent them to a page that is designed to benefit you in some way or another, then they will make you aware of their disapproval.

The only way to succeed in building up a following and benefiting (in the long term), is to take the time to contribute to those communities by commenting on other people's links, getting involved in debate, and **only posting links that you know will be of interest to the target audience**. I mean genuinely interesting. Not interesting in the sense that if they buy what you are selling it will benefit them in some way.

In particular, link bait content works well in these communities. Think along the lines of "top-10 list" or "best 8" or "worst 6" type articles. Something that is interesting but quick and easy to read and understand will work nicely.

Remember, most of the people on these sites have a dilemma of choice when it comes to choosing which posts to read. They are also looking to be entertained or informed; so if there is even a hint of marketing, self-promotion, or spam, then they will turn off immediately.

Stumbleupon

Stumbleupon (`http://www.stumbleupon.com`) has a very unique community browsing pattern. Stumblers are the online equivalent of New York pedestrians — in a hurry with no time to spare. I must confess that initially I was not too fond of marketing with Stumbleupon because while it proved quite easy to get traffic from it, that traffic maintained a near perfect **bounce rate**.

A **bounce** is a single page visit. In other words, the reader has come to the page and left without clicking on any other links — generally an indication that they did not find what they were after, or simply weren't interested. More often than not, you are going after people who are interested in what you have to say and will spend some time browsing around your blog.

With that said, Stumbleupon can still be very useful provided you cater for that community's browsing patterns. Content that is immediately appealing, very quick, and easy to understand works best. Stumblers often browse using the stumble bar (for more information, simply create an account and read up on how this works), which gives them an easy and immediate way out of your site. This means that you have to be prepared for a high bounce rate from Stumbleupon.

On the plus side, content that is interesting can generate many thousands of visits. Your bounce rate is high, but so are your traffic volumes. With just the right content, it is still possible to meet your goals on a fairly regular basis.

Integrating your WordPress blog

This chapter has until now focused on setting up your own personal social network accounts (see the exercises in the download pack if you haven't yet done this). This is not the same thing as integrating your blog with those services. In order to make it as easy as possible for your content to be shared through the major social networks, it is important to integrate sharing buttons on each and every piece of content.

WordPress.com comes with built-in support for this integration on the already familiar **Sharing** page under **Settings**.

> Self-hosted WordPress.org users should see the exercises for this chapter in order to ensure that you are properly able to implement social sharing buttons in the same way as described in this section.

It is possible to add all the major social network buttons along with **Print**, **Email**, and **Press This**. Go ahead and drag and drop each and every button from the **Available Services** section into the **Enabled Services** section as shown in the following screenshot:

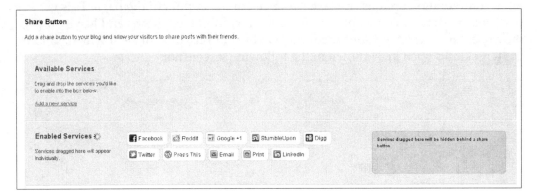

I advise you not to hide these buttons by dragging them into the box on the right of the **Enabled Services** section. Why hide buttons that you want people to use? Don't be afraid to take up a bit of space by presenting these buttons in all their glory. Sharing and socializing your content is one of the most important things you can do, so the buttons deserve the space they consume.

Once the buttons have been dragged into the **Enabled Services** section, you can drag them around to re-order them in a more intuitive manner. For example, I would present the **Email** and **Print** buttons at the end of the list, as while these are useful buttons, they don't perform quite the same role as the other buttons, which focus on social engagement. It doesn't make sense to have them floating around in random places on the list.

Note that you can also configure each of these buttons by clicking on the down arrow to the right of the service name. This configuration is the same as that used when adding a new custom social service so read that section (coming up shortly) before editing any of these buttons. By and large, the default settings are sensible and you probably won't need to change these anyway.

There is a **Live Preview** section after the **Enabled Services** section to help you decide on the order and layout of the buttons. The layout and a number of other configuration options can be customized at the bottom of the page. This is particularly useful if you want to remove the text from the buttons and leave only the icons, select which content types display the buttons, or control in which window the target links open in as shown in the following screenshot:

With social integration in place, you can be assured that your unique and interesting content will stand a far greater chance of being shared with the world. It doesn't stop there either, because there are many other social services that are not given default representation on WordPress, but are still available to use.

You might, for example, wish to post news to **Delicious** (an online social bookmarking website). To do this, click on the **Add a new service** link in the **Available Services** section on the **Sharing** page. This will bring up a form that needs three bits of information:

- Name of the service
- Sharing URL
- Icon for the service

The first and last bits should be fairly easy for your get hold of. You can always find a free icon set and upload the Delicious icon (ensure that it is 16 x 16 pixels in size) to your WordPress media and then reference that URL in the **Icon URL** section. The second option is slightly harder as you need to know what the bookmarking URL is, and how to pass the page link and title.

Luckily, most social networks have a standard way of adding new links, and WordPress has a number of variables that allow you to insert the page title and URL (amongst other things) into the **Sharing URL**. The following screenshot shows the **Delicious** service being added:

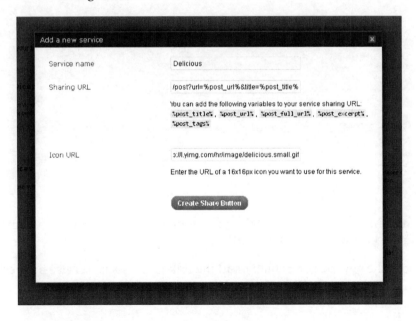

While the full **Sharing URL** is not visible, you can still see how the post title and URL were added using the WordPress variables %**post_url**% and %**post_title**% in the **url** and **title** HTML parameters. For completeness, the full Sharing URL for Delicious is as follows:

```
http://www.delicious.com/save?v=5&noui&jump=close&url=%post_
url%&title=%post_title%
```

When adding any new **Sharing URL**, you need to first find out (search on Google) which link to use in order to share content on that particular network. Often this can be found on the social network site itself as the sharing URL is embedded within the buttons they provide (this is how I found the share URL for Delicious in this example).

Once the button has been successfully added, it is now available to be dragged into the **Enabled Services** section to join all the others as shown in the following screenshot:

It is extremely important that you take a few moments to try out the new button and make sure it works as expected. In particular:

- Does the new button actually add the link to the social service in question?
- Does the new button add all the correct information?

If not, then you likely have to go back and tweak the **Sharing URL** in order to get things right. Now, when anyone happens to come across a post of yours they like, it is super easy for them to share that content, as you can see here:

Note in particular the **Delicious** button that has been added to the front of the list.

Armed with all the social integration you could possibly want, you are now in a position to leverage and benefit from social media. As you build your reach, more and more people will see your content and these social buttons will help them to pass on that information, giving you more and more benefit for each bit of content added.

Summary

This chapter served as a solid grounding in social media. In particular, you should understand how to approach each of the major social networks to further your business objectives. Along with providing useful and interesting high-quality content, it is also important to contribute to the social networks by getting involved in discussions and debates, following other people, and generally getting your name out there.

The chapter finished off with a look at the powerful inbuilt features of WordPress that allow you to integrate social sharing buttons for each of the major networks, as well as provide custom buttons for any other network you may want to use.

In particular, ensure that you complete each exercise provided within the download pack or on Site prebuilder for your particular WordPress distribution—as self-hosted WordPress users will need to install additional plugins in order to achieve the same level of social integration as WordPress.com users.

Social marketing is a very powerful tool when it is done right. By combining great, focused content and becoming involved in relevant groups and other social activities, you can build your reach. Having a wide reach will serve your purpose long into the future and can help to generate far more traffic than you would otherwise be able to muster.

5
Building Traffic III: Building Relationships

Given the sheer scope and scale of the possibilities presented in the previous chapter, one of the major considerations for any marketer must be how to allocate time. I would recommend that you consider how much time to devote to each of the activities discussed in this chapter weighed up against the benefits of the activities discussed in the previous chapters.

Not everything in this chapter may be exactly suited to your particular blog or site as, depending on your niche and target audience, advertising and press releases for example, may not be as effective as social marketing.

Luckily for you, as a WordPress user, there are a few really cool features that allow you to easily find other bloggers talking about similar things. This makes it easy to hop along, drop a few comments, make a few friends, and start integrating into the WordPress blogging community.

Remember, you aren't bound to the WordPress blogging community, and of course you should engage with bloggers based on aligned goals, shared passions, and mutual friendship wherever they may be found and whatever web platform they may use.

Contributing to other blogs and building relationships with bloggers is not the only way to generate a following and drive traffic. This chapter will also look at how to use RSS feeds, undertake advertising, write press releases and articles, as well as how best to use forums and groups.

Trust and relationships with WordPress

As discussed in *Chapter 3*, whenever you create a new WordPress post, it is possible to add several relevant tags. This is not only useful for navigation purposes (from the reader's point of view), but in WordPress there is an additional use for them.

Finding people with similar interests—Tag Surfer

If you haven't already done so, ensure that some of your blog posts have a few tags associated with them, and save the changes. Next, click on **Tag Surfer** under **Dashboard** to bring up a list of all the most recent blog posts tagged with the same tags you have used in your posts. This is a really great feature as it quickly allows you to find people with similar interests.

 Self-hosted bloggers can follow along by visiting the public tag surfer on the WordPress.com website (`http://wordpress.com/#!/tags`). After all, it is equally as important for self-hosted bloggers to make online connections.

The following screenshot shows the **Tag Surfer** page, with a few blog results based on several tags related to marketing:

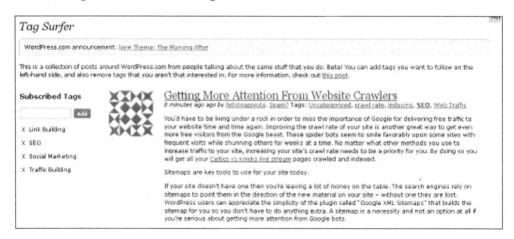

With immediate access to all the latest posts on similar topics, it is a cinch to read through any that interest you and leave some helpful comments.

Be really careful to pick and choose those blogs that you feel are of genuine quality. Regrettably, a large number of blogs are simply straight forward sales pitches. There is little point in trying to engage someone who is only after a quick sale.

However, telling the difference between a genuine blogger and a sneaky sales pitch is fairly easy. If the blogger in question is not trying to directly sell or market something each time they post a blog, it means that they are interested in sharing information and making an effort to be helpful. Also, it is quite likely that you might learn something useful from them. If you did, take a moment to comment on their site and let them know.

Commenting on a blogger's site won't make you a millionaire, but what it will do is set up a bit of **trust**. By making genuine comments that don't smack of sales or self-promotion, you build a relationship. This will soon put you in a position to approach that blogger and request a mutual link or something similar. If the other person has read your comments and been to your blog, then they are far more likely to consider any collaboration you suggest than if you go cold calling.

Dealing with other webmasters and bloggers is different from what we have discussed so far. You are looking to make alliances in your peer group.

 People only want to associate with other people they know and trust and when you are just starting out, that's no one.

That trust has to be built up by sharing content and comments, having debates, and so on.

Remember, friendships are only one way to create traffic-building backlinks from other websites. If you feel someone is talking rubbish (yes, I know… who would ever talk rubbish on the Internet), then challenge their ideas and put your own forward — preferably with solid evidence to back them up. Readers will make up their own minds about who they think are right, and if you make a compelling argument at the expense of someone who is leading his readership astray, you might just win them over to your side.

Get on the radar with other WordPress blogs

While the tag surfer is useful for discovering new posts and blogs on related topics, it is not the only way to discover new blogs. Head on over to the WordPress.com home page and browse through the posts there. They also have a **Tags** tab that shows the major tags on the site. You can use Google to search for other blogs too (`http://www.google.co.uk/blogsearch`).

Once you have found a few blogs worth following, subscribe to them (if you are using WordPress.com) so that you can keep up-to-date with what is going on in their world; you can also use RSS, follow them on Twitter or Facebook, or simply bookmark their home page.

Apart from subscribing to blogs, it is also worth liking any posts you think are genuinely useful on Facebook, or tweeting about the post on Twitter. Likes and tweets are part of relationship building as more often than not the author of the blog or post is e-mailed to let him/her know you have subscribed to or liked their content. This puts you on their radar and the e-mail also provides links back to your blog for them to check out what you are doing.

It is easy to follow any blog using the **Follow** link in the WordPress toolbar that shows along the top of your screen whenever you are logged in to WordPress.com as shown in the following screenshot:

Subscriptions can easily be managed using the **Following** tab on the WordPress.com home page:

The main point of this section is to make you aware that there is a whole set of WordPress features (regardless of whether you use hosted or self-hosted WordPress distributions) designed to make it easy for you to become integrated with the WordPress blogger community. If this sounds like unnecessary work, then you must change your mind set. **Relationship building** is an important aspect of marketing.

Pick and choose your partners carefully. Naturally, the more popular and widely read a blogger is, the better it is for you to cultivate trust with them. Bear in mind that often bloggers are acutely aware of their own popularity and guard it jealously. Don't be surprised or put off when you get the cold shoulder. It may well happen more than once.

While you won't have quite such convenient administrative features to manage non-WordPress based blogs, the concept of first building trust and then taking the relationship a step further applies. With trust firmly in place it is a lot easier to take a relationship to the next level by requesting mutual links or undertaking some other strategic partnership such as mutual reviews and so on.

Use your imagination when it comes to thinking of ways to collaborate with other bloggers and webmasters. Remember to make any offer equitable. In other words, if you want them to write a review of a service of yours, then offer to review a service of theirs.

Later on, you will find that people who have worked successfully with you before are more than happy to tweet about something you have done, or mention you somewhere without requiring something in return—on the understanding that you would do the same for them.

RSS feeds from your blog

WordPress sites generate RSS feeds for both content and comments. **RSS feeds** are a standardized method of presenting regularly updated lists of content for consumption elsewhere online. By implementing an RSS feed, you allow visitors to automatically receive links and teasers to your newest posts directly on their browser or other feed aggregation services.

Feeds have long been an established method of gaining a following, precisely because they make it easy for people to glance over a list of the latest headlines with summaries for a large number of sites without having to visit each and every website around. Many people use feed aggregation services to simply present a digest of all the latest content that they are interested in.

Feeds of your latest blog content can be located by adding `/feed/` to the end of your blog's URL on WordPress.com blogs, or `?feed=rss` on self-hosted blogs. If you add `/feed/` (or `?feed=rss`, depending on your blog's setup) after a post, WordPress will display a feed of that post's comments.

As WordPress takes care of the technical aspects of creating and managing feeds, you don't need to do much other than to let people know the feed is available. There are a couple of ways to do this, and the easiest is simply to drag an **RSS** widget (under **Widgets** in the **Appearance** section) into one of the available widget areas as shown in the following screenshot. This is used to display feed content on the site itself.

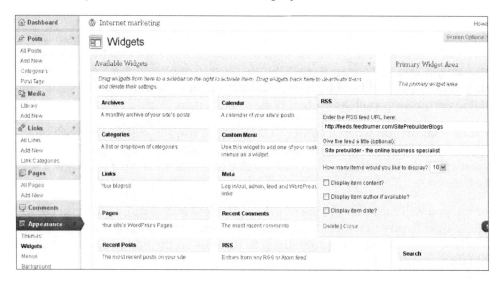

Simply enter the RSS feed URL in the space provided; this can be any feed from any site you want to include information. For argument's sake, I have used the following link:

```
http://feeds.feedburner.com/SitePrebuilderBlogs
```

With the changes saved, a list of the latest posts from the target feed is displayed on site. This can be useful for providing additional interesting information for site visitors. However, think carefully about whether or not to include third-party content on your site. It gives visitors a convenient way out, which may not be what you want if you are trying to convert traffic (more about maximizing conversions in *Chapter 6*).

What you do want, as a marketer, is for people to follow your own feed. This is also easy to take care of using the **RSS Links** widget for WordPress.com users. However, since adding prominent links that help readers connect with you is discussed in detail in the following chapter, we won't go into RSS any further here.

The main point to hold onto is that your WordPress blog automatically provides RSS facilities that allow anyone to subscribe to your feed. Popular websites can end up with hundreds of thousands of followers consuming their feeds. In fact, feeds can be a great source of revenue. Refer to the online exercises for a better way to present and monetize your site's RSS with FeedBurner.

Advertising online, articles, and press releases

The online advertising section of this chapter is going to be more of a cautionary tale than one designed to get you super excited about the potential of ads. There are a number of inherent problems with advertising online—especially if you are on a limited budget.

While I am someone who believes that there are times when it is more expedient and efficient to pay for products and services rather than trying to do everything yourself, advertising is not often on that list.

The following are my reasons:

- **Expensive**: If you have ever undertaken online advertising, you will know that on a bad day, it can cost a few dollars per click and on a good day still around 5 to 10 cents per click. That might not sound like much, but it adds up quickly.

- **Zero half life**: Once your ads stop running, there are absolutely no latent benefits. No backlinks, no SEO, no residual traffic… nothing.

- **Ineffective**: Not all advertising is ineffective, otherwise no one would do it. But from your own experience, how many times have you clicked on an ad on a website? People tend not to.

Consider the following situation with Stumbleupon, one of my favorite social networks. It is possible to run a campaign at 5c per click-through. This sends a visitor right to the page of your choosing. You might think this is a good deal, and it is, relative to other advertising methods, but stumblers stumble. They rarely stick. Your bounce rate is going to be super high as once they have looked at your page, they click the stumble button and away they go.

You are paying $50 for every 1000 visitors, but the chances are conversions are way down. Isn't it far better to write a really cool piece of link bait, and put it on Stumbleupon to let people stumble it organically? Depending on how interesting your content is, you might find that you receive far more than 1000 visits for free. In addition, you have now added new content to your site, and this can be shared on other networks, or be referenced and talked about by bloggers and other sites bringing a whole host of SEO and other benefits.

For anyone dead set on trying an ad campaign, please see the Google Adwords exercise in the download pack from the Packt site or Site prebuilder for a practical look at how to set up and run an online ad campaign.

Reviews

One form of advertising I do think is worthwhile, is a solicited online review. A review on the correct site can drive as much, if not more, traffic to your blog than an ad, especially when it is first posted and prominent on the host site. You can quote positive reviews in your own marketing material, which is great material for convincing people to trust you. Finally, reviews stay online forever; they provide a permanent backlink and lasting SEO goodness, which is not the case with a standard ad.

Paying $50 for a review is likely to provide a far greater ROI than $50 worth of ads in the long term.

 Creating your own content that goes viral is free and limited only by your imagination and can send far more traffic than any type of advertising or review, period.

Articles

You are probably just as likely to get coverage on a desirable website by contacting them and offering to write something unique and interesting. Writing an article or guest blog not only shows off your knowledge and expertise, but also provides a permanent backlink and forces you to get out there and meet the people who run these sites. This is far more useful than simply contacting their ad sales people and forking out cash.

When it comes to getting exposure on other sites, I would do things in the following order:

1. Offer to write a guest blog or article
2. Solicit a review (paid or unpaid)
3. Paid marketing
4. **PPC** (Pay-per-click) or **CPM** (cost per thousand views) ads

A word of caution is necessary when the time comes to consider writing articles or press releases. Be certain that the exposure you gain from writing the article on someone else's site is worth the effort when weighed against the fact that you are providing quality content for someone else, instead of your own blog or site. In other words, is the *reach* you gain from writing for someone else sufficient to warrant contributing to that site's SEO at the expense of your own?

If you know that an article or press release is going to be read by a substantial number of people who wouldn't otherwise be exposed to what you have to say, and that this in turn will enhance your reputation and hopefully lead to some new followers, fans, or customers, then by all means take the plunge and write for someone else.

First prize is getting an article posted on a popular blog or site that actively focuses on your niche or closely related niches. This is because the readership of that site is already predisposed to understanding and being interested in what you have to say. In addition, an article (with backlink) posted to a super popular niche website also increases your PageRank because of the new association with a highly rated website.

There are also large ezines that operate with the specific intention of gathering large numbers of article writers. Articles written on these sites have far less impact, but some people still swear by them. The best one is EzineArticles (`http://www.ezinearticles.com`).

Paid marketing

Paid marketing can be quite effective, provided you can find a good marketing person or company. Even though you are paying for someone to write content and distribute it on your behalf, you are at least free to work on your own content at the same time; in other words, you are increasing your rate of content output. Assuming the marketers are doing their job properly, you will enjoy new SEO-enhanced content that generates permanent backlinks and traffic over time, which is a step up from standard advertising.

Paid marketing can be expensive, however, as it is labor and skills intensive work.

Press releases

When it comes to writing press releases, there are a number of paid and free services available. My suggestion is that you start out using a free site, in order to hone your press release writing skills. A good one to use is PRLog at `http://www.prlog.org`. PRLog also has a number of helpful articles and documents that can help teach you to write great releases.

Forums and groups

Hanging out in forums or groups and contributing to the debate is a good way to build backlinks, recognition, and trust. It can be very time consuming and often frustrating work as, more often than not, given any 20 people, there will probably be 20 different opinions (sometimes more) about a topic that should be straightforward.

A lot of sites combat this information overload by allowing people to rate answers. This means that, in general, the best responses bubble up to the top of the list. If you are answering questions and helping people, make sure you write clearly and in a friendly tone at all times. If you are asking questions, be sure to offer thanks and appreciation to people who have genuinely helped.

Depending on your niche, you might find that there are quite a number of popular forums or groups to join, or maybe only one or two. Before joining a forum, look at what the community has to offer. Don't join a group or forum for the sake of it.

 Everything you do has to be at least as valuable as writing great content for your site! Otherwise, your time is best spent writing content.

If a group has a few hundred members and nothing new has been contributed in a few weeks, is there really much point in dedicating time and effort to it? Seek out lively and active communities and get involved there, instead.

One of the best ways to generate backlinks to your blog or site is to make sure you fill in your online profile and signature (if available) in the forums or groups. Often this info will be tacked onto any comments and replies you make providing potential fans, followers, or customers with a quick and easy way of getting through to your site.

Be warned though, each forum or group is different and has its own flavor. Some communities adopt an anything-goes-attitude and you could find yourself mingling with some very unsavory characters. Depending on what type of site you run and the type of people you want to attract, some forums and groups may be unsuitable even if they are relatively active.

When in doubt, search relentlessly for the target audience and sub-groups you identified back in *Chapter 1*, and join only those communities that are a good fit.

Summary

With this chapter behind us, the knowledge required for most of the substantial and persistent efforts you are going to undertake to drive traffic to your site or blog are complete.

You now know how to leverage the WordPress community to create relationships and trust that can help to increase your reach and generate traffic. This is a unique advantage that is made easy by WordPress.com's subscription management facility and tag surfing features.

We also looked at how RSS can help to tie people into your site by offering them an easy way to access the main headlines and teasers. Having this powerful feature automatically available on WordPress is a great advantage over other platforms. This chapter's exercises also go into more detail about how FeedBurner can be used to monetize and enhance the traffic generated by your feeds.

Advertising was given a "use with caution" flavor. Hopefully you have understood that it is important to weigh up the advantages and disadvantages of paying for advertising, and to compare that to what you are able to do yourself. We also briefly touched on how soliciting paid reviews or engaging with paid marketing services might also offer greater ROI than straightforward advertising.

Finally, we touched upon some of the main concerns and issues associated with using forums and groups to build trust and relationships as part of a well-rounded marketing campaign.

As always, ensure you have completed all the online exercises for this chapter before moving on. We are now, at last, ready to start converting and monetizing all the traffic that we are going to generate from our traffic building and content creation efforts.

6
Converting Traffic

Up to this point, all our efforts have been focused on driving traffic. With visitors arriving, hopefully in great numbers, it is time to seal the deal and convert that traffic. Recall in *Chapter 1*, you wrote down your business objectives. With those goals in mind it is time to make sure that your blog is optimally laid out and designed to maximize conversions in order to meet those objectives.

No matter whether you are selling pastries, selling online subscriptions, doing some affiliate marketing, or trying to get people to sign up to your newsletter, there are certain things that all sites need to do. That is, get first time visitors to visit again. Not everyone who visits your site once will want to buy something or create an account immediately. But, if there is a promise of valuable, interesting content they might be far more inclined to follow you on Twitter or RSS or some other social network, and eventually convert into a customer.

While encouraging people to stay within reach of your content is a generic business objective, it is important that you also have some more specific ones. We are also going to look at how to create effective **landing pages** that convert like crazy. A landing page is any page specifically designed to induce a certain action or result, in other words, make a conversion. In fact, it is not just about creating one good landing page, but sometimes a whole range of them.

Effectively, this chapter is broken up into the following two major sections:

- How to convert traffic into followers using easy-to-understand "follow me" buttons, text, and links
- How to convert traffic into customers using well designed and powerful landing pages

Remember that having followers might not translate directly into revenue, but the return from building a large following may far exceed your ability to generate revenue directly from customers. This is because followers can act like your own personal army of marketers, spreading your content around the Internet. This increase in reach often equates proportionally to an increase in revenue by driving more potential customers through your site.

In *Chapter 7*, when we analyze and refine our techniques, we will see how using multiple landing pages can help to ensure you are always using the best possible site and page design to maximize conversions.

Converting traffic into followers

Traditionally, selling products on websites could be thought of like a pitcher throwing fast balls to a batter. As the ball zips by the batter, he takes a swing. Some balls he hits, some he misses, but the ones he misses carry on past, never to return. In the same way, a potential customer visits the site and either purchases something (a hit) or leaves (a miss) without making a purchase and probably never to return. This baseball model is **not** what you want.

Instead, it is much better to think of your blog as a black hole. Each planet and star is a potential customer with a bit of money to spend. Once a star has fallen in towards the black hole, it may well miss and zip on past, but because the of the black hole's gravity, the star's trajectory will curve and fall back again. This is effectively an orbit, and what you end up with is a whole galaxy full of stars and planets spinning around the black hole with a steady stream of matter being gobbled up by the black hole in the center.

In the same way, your site might have some people who come straight to it and buy something, but most will not—at least not on their first visit. You need something to keep them in orbit around your site or blog, so that with time, they will eventually come close enough to make a purchase (or meet some other business objective). In the same way that a black hole makes matter swirl around it, you need to make sure your website keeps visitors interested enough to come back again and again.

The way you do this is by offering great content and making it really easy for people to access and consume it. In fact, even customers that do make a purchase will often want to consume content you create. Keeping customers within orbit around your site is a great way to increase the amount of repeat business you receive; if they are constantly availed of what is happening in your world, they will be the first to know of any new product, service, or offering you have.

Making it easy for people to follow you

Take a look at some of the most popular bloggers in the world, and compare their sites. You will notice that, without fail, they all make it really easy to follow them by RSS and Twitter and more often than not Facebook or LinkedIn. Look at the copyblogger home page in the following screenshot:

Notice how prominently displayed at the top right of the page is a list of large visually recognizable buttons that allow visitors to subscribe to their newsletter, RSS feed, follow them on Twitter, or like them on Facebook. Anyone who is interested in learning about online marketing can, at the click of a button, access all the latest content provided by copyblogger.

While gaining a follower on Twitter doesn't necessarily bring revenue directly, each and every follower is a potential customer, or someone who will potentially recommend your blog to a potential customer. This meets the hugely important business objective of increasing reach for the site and its content—something you must also do if you are to have any hope of penetrating the market.

As we saw in *Chapter 5*, WordPress.com has an RSS link widget that can add a nice orange RSS icon to any one of the widget areas in your theme. This is unfortunately not really suitable for our needs as we need a row of icons and links to a number of different things. In order to get a nice row of icons, we will need to write a bit of HTML code and add it to a custom Text widget.

 WordPress.org users can simply install something like the **Subscribe/Connect/Follow widget**, available at `http://wordpress.org/extend/plugins/subscribe-connect-follow-widget`.

Creating a custom "Follow me" widget

Before you begin adding the links, you will need to find and download a set of icons. A search on Google for "social network icons" should bring up some useable results. Remember to make sure that you do not infringe on any copyright conditions. Only use icons that are freely available. Once you have the icons you want (preferably large, instantly recognizable ones), upload them to your media folder on your site so that they can be referenced in the links.

For example, the following screenshot shows the **Upload New Media** page being used to upload an RSS icon:

Note in particular that the icon has been given a **File URL**. It is this URL you will use to reference this icon in the HTML that follows. Once all the requisite icon files are uploaded to your media library, you are ready to drag a new **Text** widget to the top right of your page and copy and paste the following HTML into it:

```
<ul>
<li style="display:inline;"><a href="path_to_email">
<img src="email_icon_file_url" alt="contact me via email"
  /></a></li>
<li style="display:inline;"><a href="path_to_rss">
<img src="rss_icon_file_url" alt="subscribe to my RSS feed"
  /></a></li>
<li style="display:inline;"><a href="path_to_twitter">
<img src="twitter_icon_file_url" alt="follow me on twitter"
  /></a></li>
<li style="display:inline;"><a href="path_to_linkedin">
<img src="linkedin_icon_file_url" alt="connect with me on
  linked in" /></a></li>
</ul>
```

Make sure that you change the paths in the code to suit your own setup. For example, this code used in my social marketing crash course home page on WordPress looks as shown in the following screenshot:

With the icon files correctly referenced, the individual e-mail (you can add your own contact form using the **Add New Post** page and clicking on the **Add a custom form** icon), Twitter, RSS, and linked pages also correctly linked to, you can save the **Text** widget.

You might decide to add Facebook or other icons, or you might not want to use LinkedIn. It is easy to add and remove new icons by copying and pasting additional link (`<li></li>`) elements into the unordered list parent tags (`<ul></ul>`). In this case, the resulting links are displayed on the live site as shown in the following screenshot:

OK, so the icons here are possibly a bit too small. I could hunt around for bigger ones, but it is also easy to add a bit of text to the links (after the `img` tag), or use some HTML to modify the layout to suit. The goal is to make it very easy and clear for any visitor to convert into a follower.

By prominently displaying the various ways in which visitors can convert to followers, you upgrade your blog from the old baseball paradigm to the new black hole paradigm. As time goes by, you will benefit by building up a large network of followers who double as potential customers, and an army of marketers who can spread the word about your content, products, and services.

Converting traffic into customers

Visitors to your site may arrive there for a number of different reasons. They may have searched for something on Google and, as you have been writing plenty of great SEO enhanced content, been directed to one of your pages by the search results. Alternatively, someone (generally a follower) may have recommended you to them. They may have found something you wrote in a social network or forum, or they may be responding to a press release or review about your site.

However people arrive, it is important that your site is equipped to make it easy for them to convert to customers. Either people are going to arrive at a landing page designed to get a sale, for example, if they are coming directly from a press release or some other promotional material. Alternatively, they will arrive at a piece of content and should be directed or encouraged to visit a landing page.

This is precisely why it is so important that your content be highly relevant. For example, if a visitor is reading an article on "how to bake the world's greatest cookies", it might make sense for them to see a link to a "list of the world's best cookie cutters" (which also happen to be the products you are selling). However, for this page, it is probably not as easy to direct them to a page selling used auto parts.

In effect, you have two types of page on the site:

- Standard, content oriented page—the vast majority will be blog posts designed to enhance your site's SEO and build traffic through organic search, social media, and backlinks
- Landing page—designed specifically to convert

If a visitor is on the first type of page, you want to get them to the second type of page, and if they are on the second type of page, you want them to convert (to fulfill the intended business objective, whatever that may be). The art involved here is to get people to visit the landing page without feeling like they are being pushed. It needs to feel organic, natural—as if the visitor made their own mind up to visit that page and purchase that product or service.

Before we look at how to create the perfect landing pages, let us take a look at how to get visitors from a standard page to the landing page that will close the deal. Effectively, you have to learn how to advertise your own products and services on your own blog.

Advertising effectively

There are a couple of different ways to advertise your own products or services. The easiest method involves direct linking from content. Without overdoing it and where it is appropriate to do so, simply mention and link to a product or service from the content you create. This is a particularly good tactic if your content is regularly republished elsewhere because it generates multiple backlinks directly to the landing page.

Be warned, however, that embedding links to your own products and services from within content is often construed as self-promotion and may earn you the disapproval of any social networks you spread the content on. When in doubt, leave out these links and focus on providing useful content alone. Besides, you are going to make sure that anyone who does read that content will still be exposed to your products and services.

The next method involves creating a highly visible ad that appears in close proximity to the content people are coming through to read. I should point out that when I use the term "ad", I don't mean you have to make it look like one of those gaudy, colorful banner ads that infest most websites. I mean a bit of content that accurately and clearly summarizes what you are offering. It's an ad in the sense that it directs users to a product or service, but it is presented as part of your site that is particularly useful or valuable to the visitor.

Take a look at Site prebuilder (`http://www.siteprebuilder.com`). Click on any one of the blog posts.

As you can see, the content title **SEO & marketing with hosted WordPress blogs** is the main focus of the page, with the content following below. Anyone looking at this page will immediately know where to look to find the content without being distracted or disrupted by the ads that surround the content.

In particular, there are ads about **Online Internet Learning** (light blue box on the right of the page) and course products (top of the page) as well as information about other products and services in the right-hand column (not shown in screenshot).

Everything that surrounds the content on every single content page is designed to encourage visitors to:

- Keep reading — there are related blog posts displayed below the content (not visible in this screenshot)
- Follow, contact, and subscribe — shown in the link icons at the top right (following the black hole paradigm)
- Visit a landing page — to close a sale and generate revenue

Note how the ads are all about things that might interest someone who is reading an article on blogging. Someone who is interested in blogging might well be interested in a course on how to make money online (shown at the top of the page), or may be interested in accessing a professional learning environment for bloggers, entrepreneurs, start-ups, and small business (Online Internet Learning ad).

Readers are also not pushed into clicking on these links. By the time they reach the bottom of the blog post, there are plenty of options for them to continue reading more interesting content. Each time they read something new, however, they are re-exposed to the ads.

If you are doing the job right, then the more people read, the more they get to know you and trust you because you always provide useful, quality content. The more they read and trust you, the more likely they are to eventually click on one of the ads and go ahead and convert to a follower or customer.

Like the black hole holding on to matter with gravity, you want to keep people in orbit around your site using interesting and engaging content. As they get to know you, over time, they become more likely to make a purchase or convert, especially if your products and services are closely related to the content they come to the site to read.

Finally, it is important to note that there are really two types of ads on the Site prebuilder pages. The first is a visually appealing "quick sell" type of ad shown for the courses. In this case, the customer sees a picture of the course cover (which is itself an indication of the type of content contained in the course). They see a title (a link to the landing page), a link to buy the course directly, and a quick summary.

I felt that this type of ad was suitable for a low cost, high value product like a crash course. It is something you might see and say "Yeah, I could use that right now" — like an impulse buy. I have made it easy to purchase without even having to visit a landing page to close the sale. That is not to say that there isn't a landing page for each course, there is. It is just that I know that many people will see it and want to buy without needing more info; so why force them to go to an intermediate page?

On the other hand, the **Online Internet Learning** program is something that people want to understand more about before purchasing. It is more expensive and, as a service, more complex than a one-day crash course. As a result, the ad offers a title and a brief summary of the main features all within a link to the service's landing page.

You will have to spend some time thinking about how best to present the information you want to get across to your visitors. For something simple like a newsletter signup, you can add the e-mail capture form directly to each page, as most people understand what a newsletter is already; they only have to decide if they want access to the content you are offering. If, however, you are selling something like, for example, innovative anti-laser products for the medical industry, you will probably need a good landing page as people aren't likely to buy something like this on a whim.

Creating powerful landing pages

It helps to plan a new landing page by dividing up any potential audience into three categories:

- Early adopters
- Curious
- Cautious

Early adopters are the type of people who know what they want, or are happy to try out new things more or less on impulse. These people don't want to get bogged down in details. They want to know and understand the big picture and then take action; the details will sort themselves out later.

Curious people are also open to new ideas, concepts, products, and services. Unlike the early adopters, however, they want to know a bit more about what they are getting themselves into. They don't have to know every little detail, but they are not going to jump straight in without dipping a toe in first.

Cautious people want to know absolutely everything before making a move. They will probably want to read through the entire terms of service before signing up to anything (I know it's probably bad, but I don't think I have ever had the patience to read through a full terms of service — I am probably on the early adopter side of curious).

Each of these types of people must be catered for on each landing page. On the surface of things, you might think it is more work to cater for cautious people and that it is simply easier to go straight for early adopters. The reality is that you can't really tell the quality of customer by which group they fall into. Early adopters might be fickle and leave just as quickly as they arrived, while cautious people might be more loyal and stick with you once they have made a choice... or vice versa.

The point is that it is good practice to build pages with these three types of people in mind. What you end up with, when designing like this, is a visually appealing page that makes it easy to buy, offers a bit more info (perhaps lower down the page) for curious people and makes in-depth information freely available (most likely in links) for cautious people to use.

This landing page design tactic is visible everywhere; refer to the online exercises for examples.

I should point out that there is one very important additional point that needs to be applied to landing pages — Don't introduce unnecessary distractions!

The purpose of a landing page is to convert visitors. It should only have a single focus. Don't make landing pages that meander around different topics, services, and products. It shouldn't introduce links that allow potential customers an easy way out. In other words, once someone is on a landing page, try to limit or remove anything else that is not necessary and could pull the visitor away from the primary objective of that page.

Armed with this overall understanding of how the macro structure of the page caters best for everyone, let us look at the individual elements that go into each landing page.

Headline

The vast majority of people only really skim over content. If you have ever operated an online service, you will know that people don't ever **RTFM** (Read the Manual: a quick search on Google will provide you with a more precise definition of this term, if you haven't heard it before). That is why it is imperative that the landing page header is both informative and catchy — it is what makes people stick and forms their first impression of the product or service.

The heading must be informative in the sense that it gives away the primary reason a visitor should make a purchase, and catchy in the sense that it should get people excited about what they are looking at.

Remember too that a page heading has great SEO value, so you must remember to try and incorporate relevant SEO keywords and phrases where appropriate. Check out the following two headlines that might be used to link to a book on baking pastries:

- Buy a book of my recipies
- Tasty baking recipes for pastry enthusiasts

The first headline is pretty awful because it doesn't hold a clear promise (a recipe could be for anything). The second headline is much better in that it incorporates likely SEO keywords and phrases (that is, tasty baking recipes, baking recipes, pastry) and also makes it abundantly clear what the reader can expect. It is also catchier in the sense that there is a promise of tasty treats to come. The only promise in the first sentence is that you have to pay for something.

Context

One of the fundamentals we learned earlier in this book was how to divide up the overall target market into smaller audiences. A landing page is no different. You might have written a book of baking recipes, but you probably don't want to limit yourself to pastry enthusiasts alone. What about people wanting to learn how to bake? Or couples entertaining guests who want some baked desserts?

Any given landing page can't be everything to everyone and you don't have to make it so. A landing page must have a razor-sharp focus. Its sole purpose is to make sales, not offer vague promises to a vaguely defined audience. The way to keep your landing pages focused but contextually relevant is to create several of them to cater for different audiences.

You should have no problem in creating newly focused headlines and content for properly distinguished target audiences. You can't copy and paste the content otherwise you may get penalized by Google for duplicate content. However, you shouldn't be tempted to copy and paste anyway, as you are highlighting different aspects of the product or service that are most likely going to appeal to the target audience.

Be careful though. There is no point in creating 30 marginally different pages. Only use separate landing pages when there are distinct differences between target market interest groups.

You can then reference the most relevant landing page depending on what you are writing about, where you are, and who you are talking to.

Call-to-action

The landing page must make it very clear what the visitor is supposed to do, that is, sign up for a newsletter, buy a book, subscribe to a service, or whatever. After the headline, the call-to-action should be the next most important page element. In fact, if it is appropriate, you can add several calls-to-action on the page. You will often see pages with a big "Get started" button at the top of the page, but several other links to get started somewhere else.

Don't beat around the bush, or be coy about what the purpose of the page is. Make it clear. If the visitor believes that what you offer is of value to them, then it makes sense to give them the ability to close the deal as quickly and painlessly as possible.

Visual appeal

It is really important to provide some sort of graphic content. Often a good image can do more to communicate what a visitor is looking at than any text, no matter how well it is written. For example, a professional cover, displayed prominently on the landing page makes an important statement to visitors and gives that individual book a kind of brand as well as a mental image for the visitor to associate with.

The following screenshot shows the Amazon landing page for one of my previous titles published by Packt Publishing:

In this case, the book cover makes it fairly clear what subject the book covers. However, there is something about it that might strike you as odd. Why have they added an image of a flower on the cover? After all, flowers have little to do with web development. This serves to demonstrate how you can use one of two visual methods to help make your product stand out:

- Images can be descriptive — they visually demonstrate exactly what the customer needs to know

- Images can be emotive — they stick in the customer's mind without necessarily being descriptive

In fact, Seth Godin (a bestselling marketing author and public speaker) suggests that today's products should be like a purple cow — unusual and unique. Otherwise they run the risk of being invisible.

Think carefully about the images and overall visual look and feel of your landing page. It can have a great effect on its conversion rate. Google once famously tried out 40 different shades of blue to determine which shade was the optimal one for maximizing conversions on one of their sites.

The lead

The lead paragraph is also hugely important because it is the first bit of real content that a potential customer will read. It should be written clearly and concisely to convey the main benefits of the product or service. This is written with the curious group of people in mind. In other words, don't waste time by going into too much detail. Don't make it complex or hard to follow — even if what you are offering is fairly complex or not easily understood. Focus on the benefits and interesting or value added aspects of your offering.

The lead should either convince curious people that there is sufficient value to warrant a purchase, or convince cautious people to continue reading further. Cautious people will want more detail and you can give it to them further down the page when you highlight important features or explain what can be achieved in more detail.

Here is a good example of a visually appealing landing page with a lead paragraph that explains exactly what the service does taken from the DemoAnywhere (`http://www.tryphone.com`). Note too that they display their **PMM (Primary Marketing Message)** prominently.

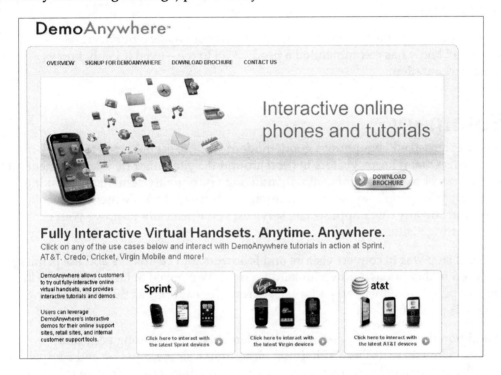

Again, writing strong leads is as much art as it is science. You need to bear in mind all the fundamentals of content creation we learned in the early stages of this book (especially SEO), but also be as compelling as possible.

Corroboration

One of the most powerful features of a landing page can be evidence of prior success. Corroborate your claims with hard evidence in the form of reviews, endorsements, and recommendations. How often have you seen a book on Amazon with an average of two stars and bought a copy over a competing title that has a five star average? Probably not often. Glowing reviews and testimonial are a great way to enhance the perceived quality of your offering.

In particular, obtaining a strong endorsement or review from a recognized source can make a huge difference. Put the review title near the top of the page, with the review source underneath so that people can easily see what other leaders think of your work.

I appreciate that getting valuable endorsements is easier said than done; it is not easy for a brand new product or service. However, make it one of your aims to secure some awesome one-liners or reviews about your offering and then display these prominently as corroboration. Even if you have to give away stuff for free in order to secure them.

From a personal point of view, I am far more likely to make a purchase if someone I know has recommended a product on to me—even if I only know them by reputation.

Summary

This chapter talked about how a good, modern website is analogous to a black hole in the sense that it keeps visitors in orbit around the site rather than letting them hit or miss, never to be heard of again. By utilizing your quality content and making it very easy for people so stay within reach of it through RSS, Twitter, Facebook, LinkedIn, and any other appropriate services, you drastically improve your chances of converting visitors into followers.

The next step was to convert visitors and followers into customers and the primary tool used in this case is a powerful landing page. We looked at how it can help to think of people as either early adopters, curious, or cautious as this informs how content is presented on site.

In addition this chapter looked at specific elements of the landing page and discussed how to craft these individual pieces into a single cohesive and compelling page that can maximize conversions. We saw how context can also play a role in how the content of a landing page can be focused differently depending on the audience.

As always, the online exercises in the download pack or on Site prebuilder provide additional practice and information on the concepts presented here and, especially for this chapter, you should complete all of them in order to get the most out of this vitally important subject.

The next chapter is going to complete the Internet marketing cycle by analyzing the strengths and weaknesses of the system we have in place, and improve on it using analytical information about the existing traffic and conversion patterns.

7
Analyze, Refine, and Repeat

I have mentioned at several points throughout this book that some aspects of marketing are more art than science. Internet marketing is a fickle mistress and perfection will always remain elusive. That is a good thing though as it is important to move with the times, to stay up to speed with new developments, techniques, technologies, media, and platforms.

More than that, however, it is important to continually assess your performance because this is what nurtures progress and learning. By always measuring the impact of what you have done, how the market reacted, and what unusual things went on, you will build up a body of understanding and experience that can then guide you in future endeavors. This in turn will mean you derive more advantage from the same amount of effort because you have a better understanding of what a particular niche wants and reacts well to.

I should point out that at no stage will you be able to write a blog post and guarantee that it will go viral, become a huge success, and bring in loads of cash. That is not how it works. Sometimes you will succeed and sometimes you will fail; experience and knowledge only tip the scales in your favor, they don't remove all uncertainty.

It is important to always remain flexible and adaptable in your approach. Just because posting to Stumbleupon.com the first few times doesn't bring any traffic doesn't mean you should forget about it. Instead, a lack of interest is probably an indication that you aren't providing the right type of content for that particular market. Adapt; try new things and see what works. Also, keep a record of your initiatives and their performance for future reference.

The primary weapon used to learn, adapt, stay responsive, and become successful is analytical data about traffic. So, how serious are you about marketing? At some point, it is going to require you to learn how to use a decent analytics service so that you can refine your methods armed with qualitative and quantitative traffic data.

Use analytics

WordPress.com has some nice stats (click on **Site Stats** under **Dashboard**) about traffic on your site. Unfortunately, those stats aren't as fully featured as other analytics services such as Google Analytics, which is available to WordPress.org users, and discussed later in this section. Nevertheless, there is plenty of useful information that you can derive by looking at the stats. In particular, you can see graphs and data on the following:

- Number of visits
- Referrers
- Top posts and pages
- Search engine terms
- Clicks
- Subscriptions
- Incoming links

This data can also be chopped up by day, week, month, year, or all time, which means that you can make fairly accurate measurements of the effect of your marketing campaigns. For example, let's say you write a blog post and share it on Stumbleupon.com and Twitter. After giving the article a few hours to circulate, you come back and check the **Referrer** stats for that day. You should see Twitter and Stumbleupon listed alongside the number of visitors referred from those sites.

It is probably best to allow a day or so for people to have time to see the article and posts. I have had articles that barely got a single visit on their first day, and weeks later started pulling in thousands of visitors.

Knowing where visitors have come from is really important as it helps you to understand what content of yours is successful and who, if anyone, is writing about your site and sending traffic.

In the same way, you can make use of **Clicks** stats to see what links people are clicking on the most. This helps you to understand how people are using the site once they are there. **Top posts and pages** also give clues to the type of content that is doing well, and can help you to focus on your most popular content to maximize conversions.

Lamentably, these features fall short of the very powerful analytical data and interface provided by Google Analytics. For WordPress.org users, however, Google provides an excellent (and free) analytics service that has a wide range of features that can help you to understand virtually every aspect of your traffic. Not only that, but Analytics allows you to build in your own goals and measure the success of your site against those goals.

 Good analytical traffic data is of vital importance to Internet marketing!

If you are able to, I highly recommend using Google Analytics, and you can install it yourself manually or use one of the popular plugins:

- Google Analytics for WordPress (`http://wordpress.org/extend/plugins/google-analytics-for-wordpress`)

- Google Analyticator (`http://wordpress.org/extend/plugins/google-analyticator`)

Please refer to the exercises provided for more information and practical experience using Google Analytics (for self-hosted WordPress users only).

If, as a WordPress.com user, you feel unable to get enough fine-grained information from **Site Stats,** or would like to be able to set and monitor goals, consider hosting your own WordPress site, that allows you to use the Google Analytics plugin. The book *"WordPress 3 Complete"* by *April Hodge Silver, Packt Publishing* provides a step-by-step course on how to do this successfully.

Using Webmaster tools

Webmaster tools is also an extremely valuable service for anyone managing their own site. Unlike analytics which focuses specifically on traffic and traffic patterns, Webmaster tools focuses on the site itself and how the content is indexed and crawled by Google, what keywords are the most popular, which search queries your pages rank on, and much, much more.

To verify your blog with Webmaster tools, follow the steps (WordPress.org users can install a plugin such as SEO Ultimate from `http://wordpress.org/extend/plugins/seo-ultimate` to do the same job):

1. Create a Webmaster tools account (`http://www.google.com/webmasters`).
2. On the Webmaster tools interface, click on **Add a site**.
3. Enter the URL of your site and click on **Continue**.
4. Click on the **Alternate methods** tab.
5. Select **Add a meta tag to your site's home page**.

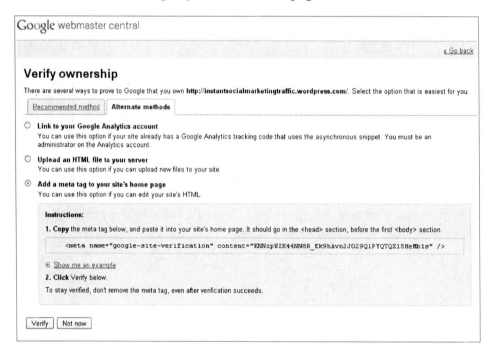

6. Copy the content key (that is, content="**content_key**").

7. Click on **Available Tools** under **Tools** in WordPress and paste the key in the space provided (labeled **Google Webmaster Tools**) and click on **Save Changes** as shown in the following screenshot:

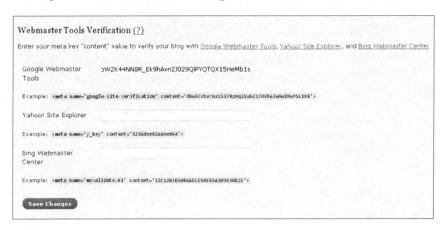

8. Return to Webmaster tools and click on **Verify**.

It will take some time before Google can gather enough data to provide anything useful so give it a week or so before you start checking back. Of real importance are the following sections:

- **Search queries** — can help you to understand your organic search traffic better
- **Crawl errors** — can alert you to broken links and other site related problems
- **Keywords** — indicate which terms Google believes are most important for your site
- **Links to your site** — shows you who is linking to your pages and from where

By regularly checking up on your Google webmaster account, it is possible to limit any SEO damage that might arise from accidental broken links that you might otherwise not find. It is also very useful for understanding how the search engines view your content and how well your pages are competing in searches.

For example, the following screenshot shows the most common keywords found on my site:

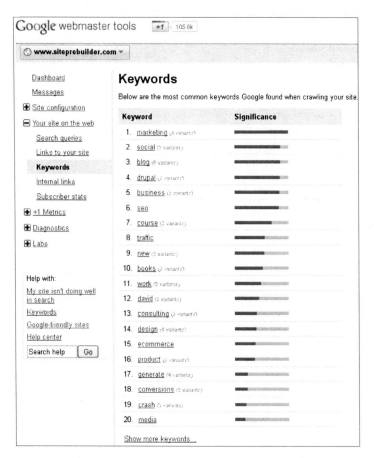

The keywords shown here are a fairly accurate representation of the site's content. These change as I write new books and new content to complement those books. As you can see, for a site that focuses on business and **marketing**, I use terms like marketing, **social**, **blog**, **business**, and **seo** frequently.

Often you will find that your blog isn't appearing in searches as well as you want it to for certain keywords, and webmaster tools gives you the information you need to see why; by carefully analyzing the data collected here over time, it is possible to tweak site content to get rid of unwanted key phrases, or raise others into prominence, and improve your SEO.

Remember, you should also integrate your blog with **Yahoo! Site Explorer** and **Bing Webmaster Center** in much the same way as outlined here for Google. Please refer to the exercises given along in the code bundle or on Site prebuilder (`http://www.siteprebuilder.com`) for more information.

The Internet marketing cycle

Once you are able to measure your site traffic and interpret it, it is time to really start marketing in earnest. You now have all the skills, information, and tools to complete the entire marketing cycle. The following diagram shows how all the pieces we have discussed in the book so far fit together:

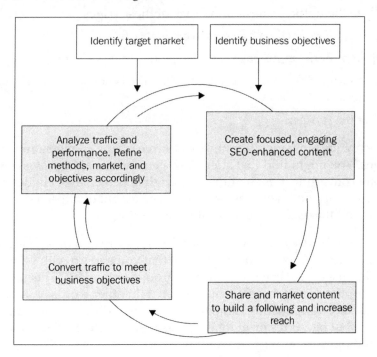

By monitoring, analyzing, and understanding your site's traffic patterns within the context of your marketing efforts, you will be able to make educated guesses and powerful deductions about what does and doesn't work well.

Implement multiple landing pages

Before we finish, there is one last trick to discuss and that is a technique used by many, if not all, of the bigger websites — running multiple landing pages in parallel. This is an efficient way to use the traffic you generate to perform *market research* and gather intelligence.

The following steps show you how it works:

1. Provide a range of different landing pages for the same offering.
2. Drive traffic to those pages using content and marketing (as outlined in this book).
3. Analyze the traffic patterns and usage of those pages.
4. Measure their effectiveness in converting traffic.
5. Drop poor performing pages and keep ones that perform well.
6. Create additional landing pages based on the best features of the previous generation.
7. Repeat the process.

Using this technique is a very efficient way to drive up the conversion rates of your landing pages. You might find that after a few generations of improved landing pages, you are converting at many times the original percentage. Higher conversions mean a greater return on investment for the same amount of effort, which means higher profits and that is the **whole point of marketing**.

I should point out that there is a lot of scope for creativity and imagination at every phase in this iterative process. You might find that you end up with permanently distinct landing pages that cater for different groups or markets. This means that your marketing efforts may become multi-faceted (in other words, you run several distinct, simultaneous marketing campaigns that target different audiences for the same product), but hey, if it's meeting your business objectives more efficiently than a catch-all landing page, it must be worth it, right?

Summary

Without analytics, analysis, and interpretation of traffic, Internet marketing is like shooting without being allowed to see whether or not you are hitting the target—you use more bullets than you need to and never improve your aim. It is critically important to know how your content and marketing efforts are affecting the target audience. You have to know who is coming to your site and how they are using it.

By understanding traffic patterns and using that information to identify weaknesses and strengths, you will be able to create targeted marketing campaigns to out-compete your competitors and drive revenue, reach, and success. Work smart *and* hard, not just hard.

You now have everything you need to become an Internet marketing champ and drive real online success. The deciding factor now, and the only thing you won't learn in a book, is determination.

I wish you the best of fortune.

Index

online advertising 61
RSS feeds 59
Tag Surfer page 56
Return On Investment (ROI) 18
reviews 62
robots.txt file 32
RSS feeds 59-61
RTFM 77

S

Search Engine Optimization (SEO) 19
about 18, 25
don'ts 37
do's 36
SEO, for WordPress sites
categories 32
document structure 33
keywords and phrases, using 30
page structure 29, 30
SEO 27
site structure 27, 28
tags 31
SERPs (Search Engine Results Pages) 25
Site prebuilder
demo 75
URL 74
site structure 28
social media 39
social networks
about 40
Digg 47
Facebook 41
LinkedIn 45
points to remember 40
social context 41
Stumbleupon 48
Twitter 46
Social Web 39
Stumbleupon
about 48
URL 48
subscription management facility 65

T

tags 32
Tag Surfer page 56, 57

target audience
identifying 14
reaching 15
target market 10
Text widget 70
traffic 9
traffic, converting into customers
about 72, 73
advertise ways 73, 75
landing pages, creating 76, 77
traffic, converting into followers
about 68
follow me widget, creating 70-72
making easy for people to follow 69
Twitter
about 46
blog, integrating with 47
considerations 46
Twitter hash tags 47

V

value 11
visual appeal, landing pages 79

W

Webmaster guidelines
URL 27
Webmaster tools
blog, verifying with 86-88
using 86
WordPress
analytics, using 84
internet marketing cycle 89
multiple landing pages, implementing 90
new blogs, discovering 57-59
online advertising 61
people with similar interests, searching 56
relationships, building 56
Tag Surfer page 56
traffic, converting into customers 72
traffic, converting into followers 68
Webmaster tools, using 86-88
WordPress blog
integrating 49-53
RSS feeds 59-61
WordPress Publicize plugin 42

WordPress Marketing
  internet marketing 9-12
  business objectives 11, 12
  target audience, indentifying 14
  target audience, reaching 15

X

XML sitemap features 28

Thank you for buying
Internet Marketing with WordPress

About Packt Publishing

Packt, pronounced 'packed', published its first book "*Mastering phpMyAdmin for Effective MySQL Management*" in April 2004 and subsequently continued to specialize in publishing highly focused books on specific technologies and solutions.

Our books and publications share the experiences of your fellow IT professionals in adapting and customizing today's systems, applications, and frameworks. Our solution based books give you the knowledge and power to customize the software and technologies you're using to get the job done. Packt books are more specific and less general than the IT books you have seen in the past. Our unique business model allows us to bring you more focused information, giving you more of what you need to know, and less of what you don't.

Packt is a modern, yet unique publishing company, which focuses on producing quality, cutting-edge books for communities of developers, administrators, and newbies alike. For more information, please visit our website: www.packtpub.com.

About Packt Open Source

In 2010, Packt launched two new brands, Packt Open Source and Packt Enterprise, in order to continue its focus on specialization. This book is part of the Packt Open Source brand, home to books published on software built around Open Source licences, and offering information to anybody from advanced developers to budding web designers. The Open Source brand also runs Packt's Open Source Royalty Scheme, by which Packt gives a royalty to each Open Source project about whose software a book is sold.

Writing for Packt

We welcome all inquiries from people who are interested in authoring. Book proposals should be sent to author@packtpub.com. If your book idea is still at an early stage and you would like to discuss it first before writing a formal book proposal, contact us; one of our commissioning editors will get in touch with you.

We're not just looking for published authors; if you have strong technical skills but no writing experience, our experienced editors can help you develop a writing career, or simply get some additional reward for your expertise.

WordPress 3 For
Business Bloggers

ISBN: 978-1-84951-132-2   Paperback: 350 pages

Promote and grow your WordPress blog with
advanced marketing techniques, plugins, advertising,
and SEO

1. Use WordPress to create a winning blog for
    your business

2. Develop and transform your blog with
    strategic goals

3. Market and measure the success of your blog

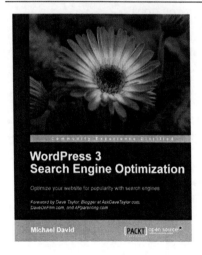

WordPress 3 Search
Engine Optimization

ISBN: 978-1-84719-900-3   Paperback: 344 pages

Optimize your website for popularity with
search engines

1. Discover everything you need to get your
    WordPress site to the top of the search engines

2. Learn everything from keyword research and
    link building to customer conversions in this
    complete guide

3. Packed with real-word examples to help get
    your site get noticed by the likes of Google,
    Yahoo, and Bing

4. This easy-to-read guide takes you
    step-by-step through the process of building
    a search engine-friendly WordPress site

Please check **www.PacktPub.com** for information on our titles

WordPress 3 Complete

ISBN: 978-1-84951-410-1   Paperback: 344 pages

Create your own complete website or blog from scratch with WordPress

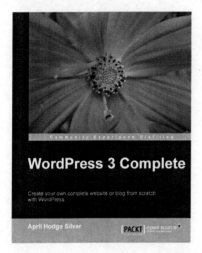

1. Learn everything you need for creating your own feature-rich website or blog from scratch

2. Clear and practical explanations of all aspects of WordPress

3. In-depth coverage of installation, themes, plugins, and syndication

4. Explore WordPress as a fully functional content managwement system

WordPress 3 Ultimate Security

ISBN: 978-1-84951-210-7   Paperback: 408 pages

Protect your WordPress site and its network

1. Know the risks, think like a hacker, use their toolkit, find problems first – and kick attacks into touch

2. Lock down your entire network from the local PC and web connection to the server and WordPress itself

4. Find out how to back up and secure your content and, when it's scraped, know what to do to enforce your copyright

Please check **www.PacktPub.com** for information on our titles

Lightning Source UK Ltd.
Milton Keynes UK
UKOW012151311012

201435UK00009B/2/P